TBH

51 TRUE STORY COLLABS

HUNTER MARCH

Scholastic Inc.

I had a hard time deciding who to dedicate this book to,
then I took inspiration from my friend and fellow author
Jenn McAllister who dedicated her book to her mother . . .

This book is also dedicated to Jenn's mother.

TABLE OF CONTENTS

Introduction

Hi! My name is Hunter March, and you may know me from any one of the thousands of videos I've put up on YouTube. Whether it be my daily news show, that time I got surprised by baby animals, or even when I made my girlfriend cry watching a sad commercial together, I've been online for a long time. And at this point I know a lot about the internet, but TBH, for a long time, I didn't know what TBH stood for.

(At one point I thought it meant total-body *high five*. It doesn't . . . because that's not a thing.)

TBH simply means *to be honest*. That one phrase, though, can be used in a ton of different ways. For example, it can be used to reveal some random thought you have, like, TBH, *total-body high fives* are basically just hugs, right? It can also be used to comment on something or someone, like, TBH, you look amazing with this book in your hands. *Or* it can be used to reveal something about yourself that you might not reveal otherwise like, TBH, I can't believe you're reading this book right now.

If you had told me when I was growing up that Scholastic would want me to write a book giving advice to *anyone*, I would have laughed, then continued not doing my homework. I used to think that giving advice was reserved for people who were perfect, and those who did things well ALL the time. But's that not true, and it's definitely not why I'm writing this. No, I'm giving this advice because when I was growing up I **needed** it . . . *badly.*

TBH, I've made some mistakes . . . okay, a LOT of mistakes. But with every one of those experiences I've learned something. I've fallen in love, been cheated on, and managed to fall in love all over again. I've been bullied, I've *been* a bully, and I've since figured out the difference between funny and mean. I've had **zero subscribers**, worked my butt off, and now I'm the face of an *awesome* company with **millions of subscribers.**

When I was younger, I would yell at girls across the playground because *for some reason* I thought they liked that. When I was younger, I would wear a beanie to bed because I thought it would make my ears not stick out as much. When I was younger, no one would ever pick me to be their lab partner because I didn't have many friends.

I know, that last paragraph took a quick turn, but *that's what life is.* It's a collection of quick turns that eventually lead somewhere great, but until you get there, the ride can be scary. And while you can't hide in a corner and avoid everything, you can be just a little more pre-pared for anything that comes up, and that's what you're holding in your hands right now (or reading via telepathic chip in your brain if this is post-2025).

TBH, this book is a collection of stories about all the things I got wrong and, most important, what I *learned* from those mistakes. Now I'm sharing them (painfully at times) with the hope that if you go through anything similar, you'll have a road map to make the journey a lot easier.

But, TBH, I don't have stories about everything that *you* might experience. Like, believe it or not, I haven't had my first period yet. And I'm starting to doubt I ever will. So it's for those stories that I've turned this book into something bigger than just me. Over the past two years I've asked my friends and fellow influencers for their stories, and now this book has become a melting pot of "Whoa! That *really* happened?"

Between the variety of people in this book, some who you already love, and some who you will soon fall in love with, there are experiences that will speak to everyone. So whether you picked this book up because of a name you recognized on the cover, because you just needed a story right now, or because you thought this was a book of total-body high fives, I hope that you can take away as much from these stories as we did awkwardly experiencing them.

Finally, books helped me so much growing up, whether it was a fictional character I saw myself in or a self-help book that answered all my questions. I've always appreciated the power of stories. Because of that, I've asked Scholastic to donate a book to Pajama Program for up to 50,000 copies of this book sold—and they actually agreed. So as you read this book, either with your eyes or that telepathic chip in your mind, know that you've given a story to someone who may not have one otherwise.

TBH means more than all of this, though. It means saying what needs to be said, even if it hurts. It means being yourself even when being someone else sounds so much easier. It means accepting everyone, holding no hate in your heart, and being thankful for the life you were given and, TBH, I know you can do that.

Thank you,

      Hunter March

1 FRIENDSHIP
FAMILY L♡VE
SCHOOL
HEARTBREAK
Hustles
INSECURITIES
STRUGGLES

Alex Aiono just got me the best friend-iversary gift EVER and now I've got to think of something to get him! What's the nicest thing a friend has ever done for you??

Lauren Elizabeth

I was really nervous that I wouldn't have anyone to celebrate with when I turned twenty-one because my close group of friends in LA are all younger than me. But all my friends from home booked flights to celebrate with me in Vegas!

Andrew Lowe

My best friend used to take me to Florida every year. We went to the beach, hung out, went to Universal Studios. Just kids in Florida on vacation. My family didn't have money to go on vacation so, yeah, this was a big deal.

Aspyn Ovard

One time I was sad, and my friend Lauren brought me over basically just this present of all of my favorite things. She's a really good friend.

Alexis G. Zall

I was out of town for weeks and dealing with some personal stuff and I didn't want to come back to LA. So I told this to a friend and we were supposed to hang out but she said, "I can't" and was super flippant. When I got home my apt was decorated and all my friends were waiting for me ♥

Monica Sherer

For my birthday, I was kidnapped.

WHAT??? 🍪

Kidnapped by my best friends! A few of them blindfolded me and threw me in the back of a car. Then they drove me up to this cabin for a weekend of snowboarding, but the funniest part is that when they kidnapped me, they handed me my favorite food: a poke bowl that made the whole car smell like fish.

Alex Aiono

Whoa, I'm really looking forward to this, Hunter!

Dang, I probably should not have included you in this group chat, lol.

Got some best friend gift ideas?
Tweet me @HunterMarch with the #TBHTheBestFriendGiftIs

The Birthday No One Came To

Before I get into this, let me preface by saying that there is a happy ending . . . Okay, let's begin.

Middle school can be awful. If you've been there, you know what I mean, and if you're there now, well, I'm sorry. It's a battlefield of insults, loneliness, and puberty. That puberty makes some students look like teachers while other kids wait patiently for a single hair to appear on their chin. I was one of those facial-hair-less kids. The hardest part, though, is that most people in middle school are still figuring out who they are and where they fit in. Some people are lucky and find friends easily, like on a sports team, or in an extracurricular activity, or maybe because they just have perfect hair. But if you're in the unlucky majority, you get stuck in middle school no-man's-land, otherwise known as the "No Friend Zone."

The only thing worse for me than being in the No Friend Zone was not realizing I was in the

No Friend Zone. Basically, I was friends with all the popular kids; they just didn't realize they were friends with me. In fact, they didn't really like me at all. But I didn't know that when I printed out exactly twenty-five exclusive invitations to Hunter March's Twelfth Birthday Pool Extravaganza!

This was going to be like one of those MTV sweet sixteen parties . . . but for a weird twelve-year-old, at my dad's apartment in a poor neighborhood, and without a Nelly performance. No one but the chosen twenty-five could come. No friends of friends, no relatives, not one person without that sweet, sweet Microsoft-Paint-designed invitation.

After I handed out all the invitations to my supposed closest friends, with a reminder that the party was at one p.m. that Saturday, I had one golden ticket left.

I forgot to mention one bit of good news: I WAS on a sports team. The bad news is that it was gymnastics. There's NOTHING wrong with gymnastics; it's just that anytime you wear spandex as a guy, you're begging to get made fun of. None of that mattered, though, because in my gym was an angel. Her name was Nikki, she competed dominantly for the girls' team, and she was ~~probably~~ definitely stronger than me. Nikki didn't go to my school and there-fore didn't know that I was widely considered a loser. Heck, at this point in the story, *I* didn't even know I was a loser.

Either way, with sweaty palms and a leotard that was probably a little too tight, I asked Nikki if she would come to my birthday party that weekend. She. Was. ECSTATIC. After I got that confirmation, the plan was in motion. She would come to my party, see how cool it was, and then in a couple of years, once we were both ready, we would get married. So I told her to be there at one p.m. sharp and, of course, reminded her not to bring any friends because . . . you know . . . it was Nelly-exclusive.

TWELFTH BIRTHDAY, PARTY DAY:

6:00 a.m.: I wake up, look in the mirror, and think, *This is it, big man. You're not eleven anymore. Time to kick some butt.* I watch Saturday-morning cartoons over a bowl of cereal big enough for a twelve-year-old.

10:00 a.m.: My dad takes me to KFC to get food for the party. When he asks how much we need, I say, "A lot, because this party might get out of hand." So we get over one hundred pieces of fried chicken and enough mashed potatoes to drown in. When the middle-aged manager asks me and my dad what the hundred-piece occasion is, I tell him it's an exclusive party. Sorry, no more invites.

11:00 a.m.: Call from Nikki. *Oh my God.* I pick up. She says she's excited and wants to confirm the address. *Hey, Nikki . . . address confirmed.*

12:00 p.m.: I string up three balloons in front of the apartment. Almost party time. My brother asks if he can have any of the chicken. No. It's for the party guests. I don't want to run out of chicken.

12:30 p.m.: The chicken smell fills the apartment and adjacent pool. One balloon pops. I think my brother did it. Never been able to prove it.

Otherwise known as the "No Friend Zone."

12:59 p.m.: TIME TO PART—wait—

1:00 p.m.: No one's here yet. Not worried, though; I get it. I invited cool kids, and cool kids are always late to parties. In fact, I'd be embarrassed for any kid who showed up right on time! Like, come on, get it together.

2:00 p.m.: Check the invitation. Address is right, time is right. Wow, did not know my friends were THIS cool.

2:30 p.m.: Nikki calls. I turn on some loud music and answer. "Hey, Nikki! Sorry, I can barely hear you over everybody in the pool! . . . You're about to leave for the party? Cool! See you in a bit!" No one is here yet. My brother eats a piece of chicken behind my back. He could've ruined the whole party with that move.

3:00 p.m.: Two hours and no one has shown up. The pool is still. Reality sets in . . . I MUST HAVE THE COOLEST FRIENDS IN THE WORLD.

4:00 p.m.: My brother has eaten seven pieces of chicken. My dad has a contagious look of worry on his face.

5:00 p.m.: The sun is on its way down. I put on a sweatshirt. I eat a piece of chicken.

5:30 p.m.: Nikki calls. I turn the loud music back on. "Hello? Oh, hey! You're at the hospital? Your mom fell down the stairs? Oh no! You're going to miss an epic party! See you tomorrow!" The one person I really wanted to show up to the party, my angel, is not coming because her mother has broken her leg . . . AND I COULD NOT BE HAPPIER! Even if she's lying to me, she still has no idea that I have no friends, and this is by far the best news of the night.

6:00 p.m.: My dad, my brother, and I have fried chicken for dinner that night. And the next night. And for the rest of the week. In my mind, this is going to be the last birthday party I ever throw, and the last time I ever eat fried chicken . . .

After my not-so-sweet party for my twelfth birthday, I hit a personal low. First I lied to everyone about how many people came to my party. Instead of admitting that no one came and it sucked, I said that two hundred people came and everyone who didn't show up sucked. But, worst of all, I realized that I didn't have as many friends as I thought. So when I graduated middle school, I made a choice. I decided to go to a high school where no one would know me. I wanted to literally just start over.

While I don't recommend running away from your problems, in this case it actually kind of worked. It didn't work in the sense that I went to a new school and found insta-popularity because I suddenly became an amazing athlete, with a bunch of extracurriculars and per-fect hair (though that would have been A LOT easier); it worked because instead of deciding I only wanted to be friends with the popular kids, I made a CRAZY decision that I should probably try to be friends with people who actually *liked* me.

See, while I was busy keeping my party Nelly-exclusive for popular kids who were never going to show up, there were probably a lot of great kids who would have been happy to eat fried chicken with me. I just didn't bother to get to know them. It took me a while to make friends at my new school, but by keeping an open mind, I found people who would at least tolerate me sitting with them at lunch. And by senior year I started hanging out with people who actually enjoyed my company. They may not have been the coolest people ever, but neither was I, and I liked that.

But I still wouldn't risk throwing more than a family dinner as a way to celebrate my birthday. Family dinners felt safe; almost everyone was guaranteed to show up. I mean, my parents had to show up. They were my parents. And my brother came . . . because there was chicken. I had friends, but the notion of nobody showing up to a real birthday party was still too real of a fear. Whenever my parents suggested it, my stomach would get more knots in it than that friendship bracelet no one ever gave me.

But nine years after what came to be known as the Pool Party of Tears, my twenty-first birthday beckoned and I had friends actually asking when the party would be. For most people, a twenty-first birthday is the best party to celebrate because you can legally get so drunk that you forget how old you are. But I don't drink. Never have, and wasn't going to start because I was now legally allowed to. Still, though, the idea of a party where people actually wanted to celebrate my birthday seemed like something worth considering. I thought, *Maybe I'll just invite a couple of my closest friends and see what happens.*

So . . . I sent out a couple of text messages. I didn't say it was exclusive, didn't make it a big deal, and I didn't promise any food. I just invited some people.

TWENTY-FIRST BIRTHDAY, PARTY DAY:

7:00 p.m.: No one's here . . . but that's okay because the party starts at eight p.m. Sorry to scare you like that.

7:30 p.m.: I text my friends to see if they're coming. I'm understandably nervous.

7:59 p.m.: I look out the window to see if anyone's pulling up. Nope.

8:00 p.m.: I stop looking outside and I turn on the TV.

8:05 p.m.: A text message. "Hey, Hunter . . . we're outside." *We're?* I open the door to see a group of five friends standing outside my door. They've got presents that I don't even notice because MY FRIENDS ARE THE GIFT I'VE BEEN WAITING FOR SINCE I WAS TWELVE.

8:30 p.m.: Five more friends have shown up; everyone is having a good time, I think. I'm not sure. Parties are difficult. But ten people were there! I DID IT! PEOPLE CAME! My mission is accomplished and over.

9:30 p.m.: Forty-five people are in the backyard of my parents' house! Who is the sketchy kid in the red sweater? I DON'T KNOW BUT HE'S HERE AND THAT'S AWESOME!

10:30 p.m.: Sixty people have taken over my parents' property. I leave with a few friends to buy something very important.

Midnight: Upward of seventy people sing me "Happy Birthday." I want to cry, but then decide not to. Instead, I go to the kitchen and grab the ten boxes of KFC fried chicken that I just went and bought. I bring it out and within minutes it's all gone! I am the happiest twenty-one-year-old in the whole world.

I promise I'm not telling you that second part just to brag about how awesome my twenty-first birthday party was (though it was incredibly awesome). I wanted to tell you that second part because I wanted you to know that if you are one of those unlucky spandex-wearing guys, or whatever the girl equivalent is, there are people out there who will like you exactly as you are. And sometimes, it's not at the cool kids' table. Being popular may look really cool on TV and it may seem really important when you are in middle school and high school, but the pursuit of popularity left me very lonely. When I stopped worrying about who was popular, who was cool, who could party with Nelly, I found real friends. I found people who shared common interests, people who laughed at my jokes, people who could teach me new things, and most important, people who would show up when I needed them. Because that's what real friends do. They show up (and they really want to eat all your chicken).

P.S. Remember Nikki? That gymnastics girl who didn't come to my first party? Well, we ended up going on a date to the movies shortly after my twelfth birthday party. I told her all about what she had missed out on, all the kids there, the chicken that people loved, and I did it all while her mom sat in between us with a broken leg.

"I'm Telling You as a Friend..."

Meg DeAngelis

Although I was born in Canada, I spent most of my childhood at the international school in Frankfurt, Germany. Whenever I mention that I grew up in different places around the world, people usually assume my parents are either in the military or they're spies. They aren't. My dad works for an international phone company. (Though someone pointed out recently that he could be a spy and that could just be his cover job, so whoa, I don't know, maybe he is a spy.) Either way, we moved all the time, and even though my sixth-grade year was going to be my fifth year at this particular school, I basically knew ten people and had zero friends. It's hard to make friends at an international school because they were moving and leaving as often as I was.

Now, in most schools, cliques form because everyone hangs out with the people who kind of speak the same language—as in, listen to the same music or like the same things. At the international school, cliques were *literally* formed by speaking the same language. Seriously.

There would be a table of German kids, a table of Japanese kids, a table of French kids, and even a table of kids from England who hung out separately from the Americans and the Canadians, of which there weren't that many, anyway. I just felt limited in the friend department. So I was super excited when these two girls, Angela and Morgan (not their real names), moved to my school from America.

You have to understand: At an international school, everything "America" is cool. It's like how in America if you meet someone from Paris, you're like, *Oh, cool, tell me things, what are the cool French trends?* But in my middle school, *Americans* were the cool foreigners. And these girls were *fresh* from America, so they knew what clothes to wear, what music to listen to, and because of their military parents, who had access to the military base, they could buy American stuff. And of all the students in the school, they picked *me* to be their friend.

They're cool, they know, they're helping me.

Angela, Morgan, and I were kind of #squadgoals for a while. They had this lifestyle that I wanted to have too. I went with what they said even when I didn't really understand it. Like, they wore padded bras and they made fun of the girls who didn't wear them. Personally, I didn't even wear a bra (because I genuinely didn't need one) and they told me I had to wear a padded bra to be cool and make boys like me—so I did it. I thought, *They're cool, they know, they're helping me.*

After the bras, they became obsessed with Abercrombie. The only problem was I had no idea what Abercrombie was because it wasn't available in Germany. So I searched nonstop online until I found some Abercrombie on eBay that I could get shipped to me for cheap. Finally I would have Abercrombie clothes just like my friends. But when I got to school wearing my brand-new outfit, they were like, "Those are the old Abercrombie, like from years ago . . ." I was so embarrassed, but instead of getting mad, I just kept thinking, *They're cool, they know, they're helping me.*

Then it happened again. I wore my hair in a new style—ponytails with butterfly clips. It took me forever and I was really proud of it. But when I got to school, the first thing Angela said was, "As your friend, I think you should take your hair down. It looks so bad. I'm embarrassed for you." I really liked the way my hair looked, but I still thought, *They're cool, they know, they're helping me* . . . so I went in the bathroom and took my hair down.

I should've realized that they were awful friends when on our final class trip to Berlin, they just pretended that I didn't exist. Like, I would talk to them and they just wouldn't respond at all. For real, though, not one word. No one wants to be ignored on what's supposed to be a field trip with your *best* friends. But at the end of the day they just said, "It was a friendship test, you passed." And then pretended like they hadn't spent the whole day being mean to me just because they were bored.

Finally, in math class one day, I just couldn't take it anymore. I can't remember exactly what

Friendship should be easy.

happened; either they said I couldn't sit with them, or maybe they made someone else sit in my seat, but whatever it was, at that moment I thought, *That's it; that is the final straw.* I stood up and said, "I'm leaving." Then I literally walked out of the classroom. I knew I would get in trouble with the teacher, but in that moment I did not care. I just wanted to get away from *them,* and it immediately made me feel empowered. Like no matter what they did, they couldn't hurt me anymore, I had escaped their meanness. It may have taken me a little while to find the way, but I escaped.

I thought it was so important to be friends with those girls, but I realized that you don't have to be friends with people just because they seem cool (and definitely not just because they speak English). I learned that trying to be friends with people for what they seem to be rather than who they are is never a good idea.

When I look for friends now, I look for people who like the real me. People who accept me with or without a padded bra, and people who tell me my ponytails with butterfly clips are awesome. But most important, I look for people who are *good* people. I look for people who don't play games, who would never try to make me feel bad, and for friends who come easy, because friendship *should* be easy. There is no such thing as a friendship test. I'm telling you this, you know, as a friend.

Be Yourself... or Felipe

It's clear at this point that I didn't have a lot of friends growing up. Well, I had some friends, just not the kind who would want to hang out with me after school, or before school . . . or during school.

These days I have plenty of friends who I love! One of my closest friends is actually someone who ignored me for most of middle school. His name is Sam. Not too long ago I brought up our previous *nonfriendship* at a party and he said, "What? I was totally your friend in middle school. In fact, I was your only friend!"

Then another girl we went to middle school with heard him and said, "No, I was his only friend." Which *may* sound like they were saying that I had two friends growing up, but what they were *really* saying is that no one could believe that anyone else would ever be my friend.

I honestly felt alone. There was one time when we were playing football in the courtyard (I was picked last) and I tripped and slid headfirst on cement (probably why I was picked last). My face was bloodied and covered in asphalt and kids just stared at me. No one rushed to help me. No one even asked if I was okay. As the school counselor led me out of the courtyard to the nurse, I thought, *If you had friends, they would have surrounded you to see if you were okay. But you don't. What's wrong with you?*

I figured I must've been doing something wrong; I mean, everyone else had friends. Some had TONS of friends. To me, the answer was clear. It wasn't them, it was me. Inevitably I started comparing myself to everyone else. *If I just had that person's clothes, that person's athleticism, that person's intelligence.* But the kid I compared myself to most often was a classmate of mine named Felipe. He wasn't a jock or some online celebrity, but he was one of those guys who EVERYONE liked. He just had this personality that people wanted to be around, and I thought it was because he was a quiet kid. *Quiet.* He was literally the OPPOSITE of High School Hunter.

Everyone else had friends.

High School Hunter was loud. Too loud for him to hear other people over his own voice. Most of his comedy routines revolved around making other people feel bad. He wasn't really comfortable letting other people shine. And even though he wasn't a track star or an awesome singer, he *had* to be the center of attention. Note: People often find that particular personality . . . well . . . annoying.

But after seeing Felipe's success with friendships during our freshman year of high school, I was determined to be more like him. I looked at the summer break as a time for people to forget about who I was so that on the first day of sophomore year they could marvel at *who I became*. My plan was not going to be easy; it was going to take dedication and perseverance, but I promised myself I could do it. My plan was . . . to be quiet. This *quiet* would lead to an air of mystery that would make people ask one another, "Have you talked to Hunter? Me neither." Or, "Did you hear what Hunter did this summer? . . . No one has."

So on the first morning of the first day of sophomore year, I tried it. People would catch my eye and I would not say something at the top of my lungs. Then at lunch, I launched my milk out of my nose (on purpose) and yelled "I'm a walrus!" And that was the end of Quiet Hunter.

Junior year I tried again. I made it two whole days before I started impersonating my teacher's foreign accent, in front of the class, directly to him. It was a great impersonation, but he was not a fan.

Senior year. I think I said a total of four words in two weeks; then I gave up and said four thousand words in the next two hours.

It seemed like no matter how quiet I'd be, no one would acknowledge what I was doing. That's when it hit me: No one notices when you're quiet. That's like the definition of being quiet.

But senior year of high school, I realized the real issue was that people liked Felipe not just because he was quiet; everyone (including me) liked him because he *listened*. I once saw a couple break up, and then each separately go to Felipe, knowing he would give them real support since he genuinely cared about them both. He was kind and made everyone he interacted with feel like *they* were most important. Even when he talked to me, he was one of the few people who not only put up with me, but actually enjoyed hearing my jokes. He knew what he was good at and everyone appreciated him for that.

Not long after, I realized I was never going to be Felipe. I was never going to be the quiet one, and I was always going to crave that spotlight. So instead of investing all my energy in being someone else, I learned how to master my own qualities. If I was going to talk relentlessly, I was going to work really hard to make sure it was funny and worthwhile.

I also learned that though I didn't actually want to be Felipe, I could still listen like he did. I realized that if I *listened* to people before talking, we would end up having these incredible things called "conversations" where I would learn about them and they would want to learn about me, and inevitably we would have more to talk about together. I also learned about self-deprecating humor (where the punch line is always yourself and no one gets hurt), and I learned about the conservation of words. I don't need to be monk silent for the rest of my life, but the less I say makes what I do say that much more important or, in my case, funny. These things combined led me to the debate team, to spoken-word poetry, and to being the host of the school talent show. The debate team gave me a place to voice my opinions. Spoken-word poetry in my English teacher's classroom led to all the different ways there were to speak my thoughts. And hosting the school talent show not only built my confidence as a public speaker, but it also showed me that my talent *was* hosting. Overall, I found places where my voice and humor were not only appreciated, but they were encouraged!

At the end of my senior year, I googled how to use iMovie and made a parody video of Lil

Wayne's "Prom Queen" called "Prom King." My friend Randy shot the video, I made fake grills that said "Prom King," and I used Auto-Tune to make my voice sound as much like Lil Wayne's as possible. I even got the oldest teacher in the school to do a mock guitar solo for the video . . . and she nailed it. Looking back now, it's remarkably embarrassing, but the kids at school thought it was hilarious, so they voted for me. I was elected prom king *because I was funny*, not because I was trying to be someone I wasn't. (Okay, technically I was pretending to be Lil Wayne, but you know what I mean.)

To this day Felipe is a close friend who actually works as a park ranger, where his quiet personality is shared among the trees and the grass and the vastness of nature. Meanwhile, I'm a YouTuber and host, where talking nonstop is literally my job description.

BEST FRIEND TAG

Monica Sherer and Maddy Whitby

1. How did you guys meet?

Monica: We were both competing in a ~~pageant~~ scholarship program in Indiana and we carpooled to the orientation together. It was best-friendship at first sight.

Maddy: We're both from the same town in Indiana, but only met once there before becoming roomies in LA. Three years later, we found out we were actually in the same second-grade class. #MEANT2BE

2. What qualities make your best friend the best?

Maddy: Moni always has my back, no matter how flat-out wrong I am. She also never makes me *admit* that I'm wrong, because she knows how much I like to be RIGHT. I'M ALWAYS RIGHT!!!

(I appreciate her patience and positivity more than she knows.)

Monica: Maddy is just the best at being my best friend. She's always there for me, she can basically read my mind, and she treats me like a sane person even if I'm acting crazy. This sounds so simple, but we're just really nice to each other all of the time and I love that.

3. If your best friend had a theme song, what would it be?

Maddy: Monica's entire "Chill Drive Tunez" (yes, with a *Zhr*) playlist on Spotify. I know nothing about music compared to Monica, so she keeps me up to date. Follow Monica's "Chill Drive Tunez" playlist on Spotify. #shamelessplug

Monica: "Clique" by Kanye West and Big Sean and Jay-Z, because she can rap it like a bo$$ and ain't nobody messin' with her clique, clique, clique.

4. What's your favorite memory together?

Maddy: We recently took our VERY FIRST EVER best friend trip to New York City, and we ATE. The entire city. You can no longer go there. Because we ate it.

Monica: Surprising Maddy for her birthday. One year I did an entire week of different birthday surprises, and she was actually surprised. Every single time. NOTE: I love surprising her way more than she loves being surprised, probably.

5. Who is her celebrity crush?

Maddy: Zedd. I don't know what it is about that tiny Russian-German DJ that turns her on so much! HAAAAA.

Monica: Maddy loves Calum Worthy. From the Disney Channel. Also, Maddy ^^ THAT IS NOT TRUE AND YOU KNOW IT.

6. Describe your friendship in emojis

M&M: 😵 👻 aka "MadMoni" (pronounced Mad-Money), aka our couple name/comedy name/rap duo name. Those two little emojis represent eight magical years of friendship, and prove that BFFs can succeed together. Boom.

7. What is the weirdest thing your best friend has ever done?

Monica: Maddy has a slight problem with her bladder and she pees her pants sometimes. Like actually full-on pees her pants. Sorry, Mad.

Maddy: When Monica laughs TOO hard, she immediately cries. Like, very serious sobbing. Then she tries to mask the cry with another laugh and finds herself stuck in some crazy laugh-cry combo. The whole situation is very strange AND YES, FINE, I PEED MY PANTS ONE TIME. OKAY, A FEW TIMES.

8. If her house was on fire and she could save only one thing, what would it be?

Monica: Her dogs. No questions asked.

Maddy: My dogs. Moni doesn't obsess over material things, so I don't know what item of hers she would save, but she better save my dogs if it ever comes down to that.

9. Show us a picture that best captures your friendship.

From left to right: Monica, Maddy

Best Friends: A Love Story

Jenn McAllister

Lauren Elizabeth and I were partners in crime from the moment we met, literally. During my junior year of high school, my friend Jack Baran and I went to meet up with our friend Alexa Losey at IMATS (the International Make-Up Artist Trade Show), or what I like to call the Beauty Guru Convention. But we didn't exactly have tickets . . . Alexa had devised a plan to sneak us in, but when the day arrived, Alexa wasn't feeling well, leaving Jack and me to figure it out ourselves.

While outside the convention center trying to come up with a plan to get in, we ran into Lauren. We recognized each other from our videos and she helped Jack and me find fans exiting the convention who would let us "recycle" their admission bracelets to get in. Except it's totally against the rules of the con to use someone else's bracelet. Okay, so it's not exactly *Bling Ring*–level crime, but it is *technically* illegal. Although she was willing to commit a crime for me on the day we met, it took a little longer than that for Lauren to become my best friend.

Finding a best friend is kind of like falling in love. You can't really plan for it. You can't just post on Facebook, "Best Friend Wanted, No Creepy Weirdos" (I mean, you can, but you'd probably ONLY get responses from creepy weirdos). It's more like one day you wake up and it's like, "Ugh, it turns out my life doesn't work without you, and not just because I steal things from your closet."

When I moved to LA I wasn't exactly looking for a best friend. I already had two, Jordyn and Gabriela. Two best friends who are also basically the two best people in the world. They're smart. They're funny. They always stood up for me when kids at school would make fun of me for my YouTube videos. AND they let me do crazy things like crack eggs on their heads for those YouTube videos.

And then I moved three thousand miles away from them, and one day I walked into AwesomenessTV and there was Lauren. She was interning there for the summer. It was like the beginning of a romantic comedy when the girl realizes that the cute guy she met on the subway and thought she'd never see again is the new photographer at her magazine, or owns a rival bookstore or something. Whenever I had to stop by the office to shoot a video, I'd hang out with Lauren at her desk. And, even more romantic-comedy cliché, we learned that we lived in the same apartment complex.

Finding a best friend is kind of like falling in love.

At first we started hanging out more because of work. We'd go to Awesomeness events together. We started carpooling to video shoots, and even though LA traffic means that driving to work is basically like an *Oregon Trail*–style expedition, we never ran out of things to say.

Since both of our roommates were in relationships and we weren't, we started hanging out more outside of work. It was never like "Hey, do you want to hang out just the two of us"; it started out more "Oh, your roommate is also ignoring you to spend time with her boyfriend? Cool. Let's go get food."

Being friends with someone new is kind of like dating: It's always totally different and risky. You never know how it's going to work out. But Lauren and I always seemed to be on the same wavelength. Like, scarily on the same length. We basically have the same thoughts. We have the same sense of humor, so probably half our time together is spent laughing to the point of actually crying. But we also have the same work ethic. Since we both make videos and we are technically our own bosses, it would be easy for us to get caught up in hanging out and not get any work done. But we are both so motivated that it's like double the motivation.

Still, when anything big would happen or I'd need advice about something, my first instinct was to call or text Gabriela and Jordyn. But asking for advice, especially when it had to do with LA things, was hard because they didn't know the whole story. When you're freaked out or in a fight or worried you just totally humiliated yourself in front of your crush, you don't exactly have the time to explain the backstories. Gabriela and Jordyn are still awesome people; I would still do anything for them. But they weren't there. And sometimes you just need a friend who *is* there.

I had a lot of friends in LA who were happy to give me advice, but it was like Lauren always went an extra step. She was just different from my other LA friends. A lot of people will tell you what you want to hear. They don't want to hurt your feelings, so they'll just be like, "You're fine, it's cool, do whatever." Lauren has always told me the right thing to do even if it was the harder thing to do. (Because as much as it sucks, the harder thing is usually the right thing.) Looking back at those times in my life, I kind of realized that whenever I took her advice, things just worked out. That's probably when I should've known she had become my best friend. But it took a big romantic airport-chase-flash-mob-at-the-train-station-kissing-in-the-rain-style scene for me to see it.

So there was this guy I kind of liked. Okay, I really liked. And he seemed to like me too. Nothing really happened, we were just hanging out, but it seemed like maybe it was starting to be more than that. Then one night Lauren and I were chilling with a group of people at one of our friends' houses and he just barged in to confront me. He wasn't subtle about it at all. He didn't even say hi to our other friends. He literally walked in and said, "Where's Jenn?" He took me aside and with no ramp-up or ease-in or polite "Hey, how was your day?" he just flat-out said, **"I don't like you anymore."** My heart dropped to my stomach.

I walked back into the room with our other friends and tried to pretend I was fine. But I was aggressively not fine. I was the opposite of fine. That's when Lauren leaped into action. She took me home and on the way stopped and got a disgusting amount of fast food. We spent the night staying up late talking and eating so much food that it's seriously gross to think about. And by the end of it I was *actually* fine. He was just a boy, and I realized in that moment I had something much better that had been under my nose the entire time. I had a best friend. There was no official conversation, like, "Hey, so you're my best friend now, right?" We both just sort of knew.

When you're growing up, who your "best friend" is can be confusing. It's easy to think that the person you've known the longest or the person that you've experienced the most with is that person by default. But when it gets down to it, a best friend is the person who steps up when you need them and you can fully be yourself around. Whether it's showing up with a cookie from your favorite bakery when you've had a long day or just being there to watch bad reality TV you don't really want to admit to other people that you like (seriously, Lauren and I watch the worst television).

This Christmas, Lauren and I finally made it official. We always watch the Kardashians together, and Khloé and Kendall have this thing where they call each other "sister." We'd been joking for a while that Lauren is the sister I never had since I grew up an only child with a single mom. So for Christmas she gave me a ring that says *sister*. Basically, Lauren put a ring on it. Isn't that romantic?

Oh, and it came with a note, a note that basically sums up our entire friendship.

Friends Who Rap Together, Stay Together

I feel like my stories about friendship thus far have been a little sad . . . Okay, sure, they've been like the first ten minutes of *Up* sad, but that's only because I've saved the happiest story for last.

About two years ago, while I was doing my Hollywood reporting segment called the *Daily Report* at AwesomenessTV, this young guy walked past me holding a guitar. Now, I don't know if you've ever seen someone holding a guitar, but there are only two outcomes. One, he plays you a song and it's incredible. Two, he plays you a song and it's awful. Either way, he's going to play you a song.

So I sat back down in my chair as someone in the company introduced him and told us . . . you guessed it, that he was going to sing us a song. So this goofy, grinning kid with a guitar walked up and, with way too much pep for the morning, asked the office if there were any song requests. So I went ahead and just named the hardest song I could think of, Sam Smith's "Lay Me Down." Good luck, kid.

Luckily, it ended up being incredible. He had come to AwesomenessTV that day to prep for his newest project, called *Royal Crush*. That young man was Alex Aiono, and that was how we first met.

While I was impressed with his performance, we didn't become best friends right then and there. In fact, as soon as he left the building I'm pretty sure I forgot his name, and I don't think he ever got mine.

Then, months later, I was invited to go on an all-expenses-paid cruise! Unfortunately, this *free* cruise left out of New Jersey in the dead of winter, but still, free is great! I was able to bring my brother, Dylan, and we met a few other influencers like Josh Leyva and David Alvarez.

We all clicked instantly, and as soon as we boarded the ship, we looked for food together. We sat down at the first restaurant we saw and noticed that the table next to us was full of more YouTubers. Meg DeAngelis, Carrie Rad, and, yep . . . you're really a fantastic guesser, Alex Aiono. And yes, I see the irony of me and Alex reuniting on a cruise ship. I watch *Royal Crush*. I get it.

We squished our tables together and started talking about everything from where we were from to *why we were on a freezing cruise ship*, and eventually the conversation got to freestyle rapping. I honestly don't know how we got there, but we stayed there.

If you don't know, freestyle rapping is like regular rapping, except you come up with all the lyrics on the spot. So, like a worse version of rapping. And surprisingly, I actually had a lot of freestyle rap skills growing up; what I had never had were people to freestyle rap *with*.

So, to the dismay of literally every other table around us, we freestyled for the rest of the dinner. Here's one of the more memorable verses that summed up our situation:

Honestly my feet couldn't be any number.
Ship like Titanic, so cold it's a bummer.
Maybe if had some PewDiePie numbers,
They would send us on a cruise in the summer.

Other lyrics involved random words we were given, roasting ourselves, roasting one another, and complete nonsense that, when rapped, is actually hilarious. Other diners probably thought we were the worst music group ever, but we all knew we had just become friends.

But after a couple more days of rapping, and a couple more nights of free dinners together, we went home. We had a group chat going, but I didn't see anyone from that group much after that . . . except for Alex. He was at my house regularly playing our family piano, shooting painful videos when neither of us had that many subscribers, more freestyle rapping, and just hanging out. Then after a couple of months, he did it; he dropped the BF bomb and casually called me his *best friend.*

Best friend? In my head that was reserved for *other* types of friends. Friends with years of memories together, friends who had secret handshakes and knew each other's food orders, friends whose parents were friends with each other! I just couldn't imagine myself having a real best friend. So after he said it, I just replied, "You are!" which made zero sense, but it gave me time to process.

Alex was *technically* my best friend, as in, out of all my friends, he was the best one. But in my life, that's an easy category to win. I also felt like I didn't have to pretend to be anyone else when I was with him. Like I didn't have to pretend to like sports, or pretend that I was smarter than I was; he just accepted me for me. And he felt the same way. He was also down for anything. I could say, "Want to fill a pool with two hundred pounds of ice and go swimming?" And he'd say yes. (In fact, he did say yes, and we did do that.)

Also, he was kind to everyone in my life, from my brother to my girlfriend and basically my entire family. It's just who he is. He's the type of guy to ask you when your birthday is, save the date in his phone, and set a notification for a month before so he can start planning it.

Most important, though: the freestyle rapping. Nothing feels more vulnerable than letting your brain spit out words without a second to filter them. And we did that constantly. I had seen his happiest thoughts, and his darkest, without filter. And he had seen mine, and for some reason we still wanted to be around each other all the time.

A few days after the *best friend* mention, Alex and I were shooting a video together where . . . *are you a psychic?* Yes, we freestyle rapped. And although we never released the video because the rest of it was truly awful, there was one moment I'd like to share. It was small—I didn't even think about it—but in the midst of our epically bad freestyle, I rapped that he was my best friend, and for this story, that is the end.

. . . That rhyme at the end was a freestyle; I did not plan that.

THINGS YOU CAN ONLY DO WITH YOUR BEST FRIEND

1. Come over without calling. Or texting. Or knocking.

2. Send a late-night text spree without them thinking you're crazy. Even when you are being crazy.

3. Instagram stalk your old crush to make sure his/her new bae isn't as cool as you. Don't worry. She/he is not.

4. Snapchat pictures of weird moles and freckles.

5. Eat an egg salad sandwich. Have you ever watched someone eat an egg salad sandwich? It's gross. Only your best friend needs to see that.

6. Tell the hard truths. That shirt DOES make you look like a banana.

7. Freestyle rap for hours. Or maybe that's just me and Alex Aiono.

8. Have full conversations without speaking any words.

9. Take down three boxes of Girl Scout Cookies and never speak of it again.

10. Remember everything about them. Even some things they've forgotten . . . and never wanted to think about again.

What are some things you only do with your best friend?
Tweet me @HunterMarch with the #TBHThingsIDoWithMyBFF

The One

Alex Aiono

I've never been the type of guy to just date around endlessly. I see people who can do it and, I guess while a part of me wishes I could be that casual in relationships with girls I meet, it's just not me. I'm much more of a relationship guy. Of course, my struggle is that I believe in love. Laugh if you want. But as an artist, I write about love, sing about love and that's real to me, even if it's not as exciting as swiping my finger one way or another on a dating app. If I'm into you, you become my everything. When I meet someone I like, I automatically start wondering if she's the one. That's usually the moment that a true friend like Hunter will pull me down to earth and ask me what her middle name is . . . MOST OF THE TIME I KNOW IT. But he's right. I fall fast and Hunter constantly gives me a hard time about it.

Of course, the risk you face in relationships is a similar risk you face being an artist. Sometimes to create something great, to feel something great, you have to wear your heart on your sleeve and put your heart out there, which makes it that much more vulnerable to being broken. That's what happened with this one girlfriend. Let's just call her 😵.

When I first started talking to 😵 she played hard to get. For example, I might wake up thinking about her and send a sweet good morning text, and then two days later I'd get a "been a while!" Weeks of me wanting to double text her went by, and then, magically, we actually start dating. It was incredible. (At least, I thought it was.) We shared the same values (But did we?). I got along with her family. (But was I really marrying her?) I liked her so much I even went to SoulCycle classes with her. **I hate cycling.** (The things we do for "love.") A few weeks later my calves looked great, but the sleeve where my heart was needed

"Welp, I guess you're going to be single forever!"

ironing . . . I wasn't doing so well. The relationship was spiraling into a cyclone of texts and quests and I had this constant feeling that I was more invested in it than she was, that I was auditioning to play the part of . . . myself.

To get my mind off of 🌚, Hunter took me out for a day of excitement. That excitement was rock climbing. And not the indoor-gym-with-cute-colored-walls kind of rock climbing. We were on a freaking mountain. It was legit rock climbing. Oh, and did I mention that I'm terrified of heights? It for sure got my mind off of everything mostly because I was kind of focused on not dying (a slight distraction).

After a few hours of climbing (and pretending that I wasn't dangling from death 40 feet in the air), I sat down on this rock at the base of where we were climbing and checked my phone. That's when I saw it. The text bomb. 🌚 sent me a text saying "I think it's best if we end things and stay friends." . . . Even the way she said it, like it was a copy-and-paste breakup text, really sucked.

I felt like I fell that 40 feet, all while sitting down.

I was devastated inside but we do what we do. You kinda say a loud, "Okay, then" and keep it moving. But that didn't really fly. I lasted about 30 seconds and then Hunter knew. Friends know those things. Family you're close to know. Plus, I've got THREE sisters (which is like having three relationship life-coaches all around you at all times). A meal with my family is like I'm a guest on The View-Aiono edition. But I digress.

Now, most of the time when you've been dumped, a friend will console you, be sad with you, give you the time you need to heal. Show up with the aggressive tweet or post that calls the person out without saying who, etc.

"If you are not real in love, then you are not real in life. #Alexisthebest"

But Hunter didn't do that. He immediately started cracking jokes, and he was ruthless, but right.

So I got up and I climbed.

The first thing he said once he found out was, "Oh that sucks . . . you know, because you said she was *the one* . . . Welp, I guess you're going to be single forever!" Then he went up for another climb. It made me laugh at myself and Hunter kept going.

"Hey, there are other fish in the sea. But right now, unfortunately, you are on a mountain."

While sitting right next to me, he sent me a text saying "I think it's best if we aren't friends anymore either. You're kind of a downer."

After talking about it for a bit, Hunter finally said, "You know where your ex-girlfriend isn't? On top of that freaking mountain." So I got up and I climbed. It completely got my mind off of that situation, and mostly replaced it with terror, but then that intense sadness turned into a feeling of accomplishment. I crushed that mountain and never looked down . . . or back.

Instead of letting me wallow and eat ice cream and all the things people usually do when they get their heart broken, Hunter made me laugh my way through it and it helped me to climb my way out—literally. Hunter hit me with the best gift possible when things don't go your way: perspective.

By the way, SoulCycle was the perfect analogy for that relationship. You feel like you're going somewhere. You're pedaling your butt off. You're working hard but when it's done, you didn't get anywhere . . . but you did spin your wheels a lot.

When things don't go your way, find perspective from a friend who can make you laugh and remind you that these moments are fleeting. That said, I'll never give up on love. Only SoulCycle. I'm kinda done with that.

FRIENDSHIP

② FAMILY LOVE

SCHOOL

HEARTBREAK

Hustles

INSECURITIES

STRUGGLES

Why is your mom the best? Well, second best. Because, you know . . . my mom exists. 😳

Meg DeAngelis
My mom's THE best because she literally loves me even though I'm an evil child.

Alexis G. Zall
My mom taught me how to be strong. She taught me that getting nervous before things happen is ridiculous and I never thought to question it.

Andrew Lowe
Because I have two of them.

That's, like, the best situation ever.

Claudia Sulewski
My mom's the best because of her carefree attitude. Beata CAN'T be tamed, but in the best way possible.

Maddy Whitby
My mom has always made it okay for me to be honest with her, so I haven't felt the need to keep anything from her or sneak out or anything like that. Plus, she tells me when I need lip gloss. Respect. 💄

Alex Aiono
My mom has never put herself before me, or anyone! She's always made sure I'm doing all right and have everything I need.

Katherine Cimorelli
My mom homeschooled me and my ten siblings; do you know how hard that is?

Ryan Abe
My mom was the best because she put up with me with a smile on her face when most people would have wanted to put me up for adoption and she was the one going along with my weirdness and my quirkiness.

All right, after reading this, maybe we all have the best moms in the world . . . but my mom is still the best.

My Best Friend

My best friend and I had very different lives growing up. I grew up with a father *and* a step-father who loved me. My best friend's father passed away when she was just nine years old. I had a mother who made sure I was as successful as I could be. Hers didn't care if she went to school or not. I had every opportunity in the world. She had none.

After her father passed away, my best friend's mother became a functional but mean alcoholic. Her mother went to work every morning and went straight to the bar afterward, where my best friend and her sister would meet her after school. They'd sip from mocktails with umbrellas as they watched their mom transform night after night. Her words began to slur, her steps became uneasy, and her eyes searched for someone she could take her pain out on.

Then my best friend and her sister would get into a car that swerved all the way home. Their mother once drove them right off the freeway. Luckily, they all walked away uninjured.

I had every opportunity in the world. She had none.

My best friend had zero supervision growing up. No one looked over her shoulder as she did homework. No one noticed how late she stayed out. *No one cared.* So my best friend did it all herself. In between going to the market to buy more alcohol and cigarettes for her mother, she graduated high school with straight As and put herself through college.

When my best friend was in her twenties, her mother was diagnosed with lung cancer, and passed away shortly after.

I never had the chance to meet my best friend's mother, but it's safe to say that she left us with an incredible daughter. A daughter who started her own business, who never let anyone tell her that she couldn't do something, a daughter who ended up raising me.

This best friend is my mom, Sandy. She's raised my brother and me with such care and attention that we had no choice but to become as happy and successful as we've ever wanted to be. She gave us every opportunity in the world, because she knew how hard it was not having them.

What My Mom Would Want

Ryan Abe

I was ten when my mom was diagnosed with cancer. Luckily, I was raised in a really good family where my mom and dad never let fear cross my mind. They just didn't let me be scared. I think they thought if there was any kind of mental countdown, it would ruin my childhood. So until I was fifteen it seemed like it was just a part of life—but not my whole life. You know, like, *My mom has cancer but it's fine and she gets these treatments and she gets better.* I started thinking that it was something she would just live with forever.

My mom was amazing. She was the most politely obnoxious person in the world. In a grocery store line she had to speak to *everyone*, and I mean *everyone*. She'd ask them what they got, what their families were like, what coupons they had, and what coupons they needed. She was just so happy to talk to people. My dad was always quieter. When we would go out she would do the talking for him and then some. And it wasn't like something hit her when she got cancer; she was always like that. Even when she got cancer she said she felt blessed. She had a healthy family, a healthy relationship. She loved to watch *Oprah* and *The View* and laugh alarmingly loudly. It was hard not to think she's going to keep going. *She's going to keep laughing.*

When I turned fifteen, that all changed. I was in the car on the way home from soccer practice and my dad was talking about college and typical things about a high school kid's future. That's when he brought up graduation. I remember he said, "Look, just prepare yourself mentally in case things don't go the way you worked out in your head." He told me to be prepared that my mom might not be there with me. He said she could be in the hospital and unable to attend. Even then I couldn't really process that she could be gone, but it was the first time I thought maybe things weren't going in the direction I had hoped.

See, I wasn't stupid. I knew that with cancer, sometimes people don't get better. But I had built this gigantic emotional wall to protect myself. I told myself, *If I don't think about it, it won't happen,* like it could be a self-fulfilling prophecy. But after that conversation in the car, I started to tear down that wall, brick by brick. I started to have little glimpses of what things could be like. I still held on, telling myself to *be positive. Nothing is confirmed. This is just a sign that life isn't always how you plan it.*

Even though the wall began to slowly chip away, it never fully broke down, because a part of me always believed she could beat it. Every time something really bad happened, she would just beat it. She'd get sick, she'd get a new treatment, and then she'd beat it. Plain and simple. My mom was tough. Like I mean really, really tough. So tough that she once had a broken femur and didn't even know it. That's why, even a year after that car ride when my dad told me to prepare myself, I couldn't help but think, *You know what? She's going to beat this.*

Then in one week, everything changed. It was a bizarre week because it started out with just a normal thing: My mom was in the hospital. She would be in the hospital at least once a week for treatments and consultations, just seeing what stuck. She wasn't feeling well, she had a cold, nothing crazy, and it seemed normal. Then that cold turned into pneumonia. And I didn't realize that pneumonia *and* cancer can be a very bad thing.

The next day my grandfather picked me up from school for the first time in a long time. And usually when he picked us up he would be playing the same Frank Sinatra songs. But this time there was no music. No happiness. Just an alarming quiet. We knew things were bad.

But the next day my mom started recovering yet again, and it looked like she had beaten it once more. I even stayed home "sick" the next day just to see her when she got home. But when I woke up and came downstairs, I found my dad crying on the floor. I'd never seen him that emotional, and it terrified me. That's when he sat my brother and me down. He told us things had taken a bad turn. We would have a week to hang out and enjoy the rest of my mom's life, but that she wasn't going to make it past that week. That was a moment and day I can never forget, no matter how hard I've tried.

The next day my cousins came over and everyone was a wreck. I just kind of sat on the floor for, like, two hours. Silent, without any thoughts. It was like my brain needed to shut down because it just couldn't process what was actually happening. I looked at the clock and it was five p.m. and then I looked again and it was seven p.m. It was very weird; it's something that has never happened again. I tried very hard to step up for my family, and when I was around my mother I tried not to show that I was deeply upset. Because I knew that if I was upset, she would get upset. And, as much as I could at sixteen, I tried to hold my composure.

We spent a week or two at hospice, a place where people go to pass away that's nicer than a hospital. It was a weird environment. You basically walk these hallways looking into rooms of people that you know are going to die, on the way to see the person you're there for. When I got to her room, my mom and I listened to James Blunt. Even on her deathbed she joked around with me. One of the songs on his album said the F-word and she messed around with me, saying, *I should have gotten the parental advisory version*. Little moments like that were nice because it was just me and my mom; it felt normal.

I specifically remember this conversation I had with my mom. She told me, "You can be sad for a couple of weeks. But I'm not going to be happy if this ruins you, if this drags you down; that's not what this is about. You're sixteen, and I raised you better than that." It was her way of saying *this is going to suck*. But she knew me better than anyone and knew that I would be okay. I feel like she wanted to give me something like a quote to remember in the future; if I was ever down, I could think, *This is not what she would want*.

And then she passed away.

— ● —

After something like this happens, your friends and family surround you with support. Your whole family, people you haven't spoken to in years, are suddenly at your door. There are gifts. There's food just everywhere. There's so much love it's almost overwhelming.

Then a couple of weeks go by and you see less family. The phone calls stop. There's no one at the door. There are no more home-cooked meals. You've gone from zero to a hundred back down to zero and it feels awful. It's like you know people love and support you but after a couple of weeks they have to go on with their lives; they just have to. Your aunt can't just stay and cook you meatballs every day. It was hard to come to that realization, really hard.

Around that time is when I found YouTube. Amid all the sadness, YouTube gave me a place where people were always there and happy. I remember one day watching a Bo Burnham video and just laughing hysterically. It was a nice and almost forgotten feeling. I hadn't laughed like that in what felt like forever. I realized then that this was a community I wanted to be a part of. In 2008, I started uploading my own videos, and it got me really invested in something. It was nice to feel passion again; it was this new thing and it felt fresh, and after you go through something traumatic it's nice to feel that.

The first time I ever brought up my mother's death in a video, I made a video called "My Mom" and I talked about it, and I cried. When I was editing, I thought, *I look like a fool, I look like an idiot, I shouldn't upload this* because I had never made videos like that. But I did it anyway, and the response I got was incredible. Specifically, I kept getting messages saying, "You've helped me so much." And as I read them, I thought, *Really? That really helped?* The comment that really stuck with me, though, was like, four paragraphs from a girl who had lost her father. She just said that my video was everything that *she* had wanted to put in a video but was too afraid to say, and she wrote, "Now I feel like I can." To think I could possibly have made a change in somebody's life was actually insane. I felt like I was able to turn my sadness around by making other people happy. And as I was doing it, I thought, *This is exactly what my mom would want me to do.*

When someone loses a loved one, the ensuing sadness makes a lot of people want to give up. But you can't just give up. That person wouldn't want you to. My mom always believed I could achieve way more than I *ever* thought I could. Without her here, I have to do all that believing myself. What I learned from losing my mom is that you've got to live *for* that person. She gave me a reason to strive, to do better, to work for something. I'm not saying death is a positive thing, but finding something to live for can be. My mom helped me find that. She made me a better person when she was alive, and she's continued making me a better person since.

FAVE SIBLING TAG

Dylan March and My ~~Dumb~~ Awesome Brother

1. What do you guys have in common?

Hunter: I used to think the only thing we had in common was our parents. But we ended up being very alike and, now, the only difference is our eye color.

Dylan: Agreed. I have perfect sweet, blue eyes.

2. Who would win in a fight?

Dylan: Most people would beat Hunter in a fight.

Hunter: Next question.

3. What habit of your brother's annoys you the most?

Dylan: I think his girlfriend would agree with me on this one: Hunter has an insatiable desire to correct people on things he has no knowledge of.

Hunter: He ended that sentence on a preposition . . . that's annoying.

4. Where do you think your brother will be in ten years?

Dylan: With the direction that Hunter is heading now he is destined to be a great talk show host. Either that or he ages out of this line of work and becomes a stay-at-home dad.

Hunter: Give me a map, a dart, and a blindfold. That's as good a guess as any for Dylan.

5. If your brother were an animal, what animal would he be and why?

Hunter: Since he travels so much, probably a roaming animal that mostly does nothing all day. I call it a Dylan.

Dylan: He would be a six-month-old Jack Russell terrier. We had one when we were kids and it was a nonstop attention-seeking, wall-bouncing maniac, all packed into an adorably small and frail package.

6. Funniest memory?

Hunter: We've had plenty of crying-laughing moments, and they usually revolve around messing with our parents. One time I tipped my stepdad's canoe over.

Dylan: You did that to me. Not to Mickey.

7. What's your favorite thing about your brother?

Hunter: That no matter what, he'll always be there for me. Even if he's on an island in the South Pacific, he'll be there.

Dylan: When we go out to get food he will normally pay.

8. What is the best lesson your brother taught you?

Dylan: That hard work pays off.

Hunter: That not working looks like so much fun.

9. Show us a photo that you think describes your brother.

Hunter:

Dylan: Agreed.

My Two Dads

When I was four years old, before I even had the ability to retain memories, my parents got divorced. So for better or worse, I've never experienced that *traditional* family—you know, the whole white-picket fence, game nights, and Taco Tuesday kind of family. Not long after the divorce, as my dad likes to remind me, my mom remarried a man named Mickey. They had known each other since they were children, and when they got married, he brought three new brothers into the equation. He also brought a bunch of new rules that made his household and my father's household very different.

I stayed at my mom's house during the week when I was in school. That meant homework every night for a couple of hours, going to sleep at nine p.m., and waking up early so they could take me to school before they went to work.

From left to right: Mickey Lee, Jeff March

Then there were weekends at my dad's house. Literally no responsibilities. The only rule was, don't break anything, but also, we all played baseball inside the house. We went to bed whenever we were done playing, and we woke up whenever we were done sleeping.

In my mind, my dad was the epitome of cool. He yelled at other drivers, which made us laugh, he was a better athlete than anyone I knew, and he was just like a bigger version of me and my brother. He gifted me a sense of humor that led me to my dream career, and his constant support gave me enough confidence to pursue that dream. He made every weekend an adventure, either by playing sports with us for hours or by taking us to Venice Beach. For those who might be confused, Venice Beach is nothing like Venice, Italy. Venice Beach is weird, crazy, and covered in tattoos. Venice, Italy, is refined, expensive, and full of good food. Venice Beach was my dad, Jeff. And Venice, Italy, was Mickey.

There were other differences too. With my mom and Mickey, we lived in a two-story home, in a gated community with a giant, private pool, and its own park right next to it. On the weekends I lived with my dad in a tiny apartment, with a small, overcrowded pool, and one of the most dangerous parks in California across the street. My mom would often call at five p.m. to make sure we were back in the house before dark, to which we'd all say yes, then continue playing soccer until the lights went out at ten p.m.

The vacations were also drastically different; with Mickey it was cruises to the Caribbean, and with my dad . . . well, it was the park across the street. But honestly, me and my younger brother, Dylan, loved that as much as any cruise.

We never cared about the difference between our households, but it weighed heavy on both sides of my family. My mom and Mickey never wanted to be known as the strict *do your homework parents*, while my dad never wanted us to think he couldn't give us the life we wanted. And so weekend after weekend he did give us that life, until he crashed his motorcycle.

I was eleven years old when I watched as my dad was airlifted off a dirt bike track with seven broken ribs, two punctured lungs, two broken collarbones, a broken shoulder, nerve and brain damage, and a very good chance of dying. At the time, I was almost too shocked to be terrified. I remember when I first saw him at the hospital, he woke up and asked me how he had gotten there. I told him he was in a motorcycle accident. Then he closed his eyes, and a few minutes later he woke up to ask me again how he had gotten there. While he was on life support, a priest was called in for the first five days of his stay in the intensive care unit, the hospital thinking that each would be his last. After twenty-two days of the ICU and another few weeks in the hospital, he asked to be released before he was ready. He just couldn't afford the hospital, but he also couldn't take care of himself at home alone. That's when Mickey stepped in and offered to take care of him while he recovered.

For the next month, my dad lived in his ex-wife's home, while his ex-wife's husband made sure he didn't die. Mickey, who I was learning was the nicest man on earth, made a bed for my dad, fed him, and even bathed him. They had always been friendly with each other, but that was the moment I like to think they became best friends. Once you sponge-bathe some-one, you're BFFs for life. That's the rule.

Sure, I may not have a traditional family, or even a normal one. But I know that I have an incredible family. We would do anything for one another, like literally anything, and our parents would do anything for their kids. I know my parents love me with all their hearts, and with mine, I love my mom, my dad, and my dad.

The Little Sister

Dani Cimorelli

I'm not really sure how to start this, so I guess I'll just tell you who I am. My name is Danielle Nicole Cimorelli, and I was born on June 15, 2000. Also, I like honeydew melon and hate long movies. Now that we're acquainted, I'll tell you a little bit about what my life was like growing up.

I was born the eighth child into my family of eleven kids: three brothers below me and five sisters and two brothers above me. Naturally, I was given a lot of attention from my older siblings growing up; they would dress me up and take pictures of me (I wanted to be a model so bad when I was little), take me out for ice cream, help me with my schoolwork, and do all the things that older siblings do. However, I wasn't the center of attention 24-7, and the moments when I was alone to reflect on myself were not the best.

From left to right: Amy, Christina, Lauren, Katherine, Dani, Lisa

Sometimes, I would feel lost in the chaos of so many kids. Even though I was one of the loudest, I felt the most invisible. I didn't feel like my own person until I was thirteen years old and I dyed my hair for the first time. To make myself stand out from the crowd, I started searching for everything inside of me that was NOT like my older siblings, and I put it out there. When my sisters had brown hair, mine was red. When they dressed in pink, I wore black. I guess I got a little too into being different sometimes, and I wound up feeling even more alienated from my siblings. I realized that by trying to be too different, I was actually not being myself.

My sixteenth birthday passed just recently, and I've noticed that I have a newfound confidence. Something changed in me, and I've become content with who I am. While I appreciate my differences, I've realized that it's okay to be similar to my sisters sometimes because that's the real me. I could copy everything my older siblings do, but who I really am never changes. My unique personality never goes away, and that is a beautiful thing that I hope every youngest sibling realizes one day.

I may be one of the babies of our family, but I no longer feel invisible—not because I'm different from my older siblings (even though I totally am), but because I put something out there that nobody else has: the real me.

Say You're Sorry

Lauren Cimorelli

I am the seventh child out of eleven, so I'm almost the exact middle child. I think this automatically makes me the peacemaker out of all of us. And in a family of eleven siblings, there is often some peacemaking to be done. I think a big reason a lot of siblings don't get along is because they don't know how to communicate that they're upset, and they don't know how to respectfully acknowledge that they've upset their sibling and apologize for it. It's really hard to swallow your pride, realize you did something wrong, and apologize for it, but it is so important to be able to do that.

I remember one time a few years ago, I was probably about thirteen and Dani was eleven, and she had just gotten these clip-on earrings and she was really excited about them, but I thought they were weird so I put one in my nose as a nose ring, thinking it would be funny. But Dani did NOT think it was funny at all. She chased me out of the room we shared and locked the door. I was just laughing because I thought it wasn't a big deal and that she was being so dramatic, but after, like, five minutes, she still wouldn't open the door and I realized she was actually really upset. So I went and got my iPod and speakers and I lay on the ground and played breakup songs like "We Belong Together" by Mariah Carey and sang them through the crack under the door. After, like, three songs, she opened the door laughing, and even though she was still kind of mad, I said I was sorry and everything was fine.

Apologizing can be hard because most of the time it's not just you in the wrong; your sibling might be being rude too, but you have to realize if you did anything at all wrong, you should still apologize.

But as hard as apologizing is, I think it's even harder and maybe even more important to tell your siblings when they've hurt your feelings. If you attack them and make it this big over-dramatic thing, they're not going to listen. Believe me. Just like you wouldn't listen if they came to you like that. But if you calmly say, "Hey, you're really hurting my feelings right now. When you say (insert mean thing), it makes me feel (insert appropriate emotion)," it can be really effective. Most of the time, your siblings don't even know that they're hurting your feelings, and they probably don't want to, so go easy on them.

Stuck in the Middle

Amy Cimorelli

When I was growing up, I **hated** being a middle child. It was never really clear to me where I fit in. I have always been an extrovert, which means I'm outgoing, expressive, and I get energized by being around other people. As you can guess, my eleven-sibling family has a mix of so many different personalities, but most of them were quieter and more reserved than me. As an extrovert surrounded by introverts I just assumed I was *wrong*, defective. Ironically, even though I was an extrovert, I spent a lot of time alone.

All I wanted to do when I was younger was hang out with my older siblings, but I was always a step behind. Like, every year, all the older kids got to go to Six Flags Marine World. All I wanted to do was go with them, but I was too short to ride any of the rides. I was so freaking short. And since most rides had a stupid, unnecessary cutoff height, I had to stay home. By the time I was finally old enough to go, they had all stopped going.

I should have been in the middle group, but I didn't fit in there either. We were just so different. Alex and Lauren were like a team. They liked playing outside in the dirt, and I was not down for that. I liked playing soccer, but no one wanted to play, so I spent a lot of time alone kicking the soccer ball by myself. I felt very isolated.

It wasn't until I got older that I realized that there were benefits to being in the middle. I didn't have to go through everything first, or wait to be last. When you have older siblings, they get to figure it all out and then tell you what to do.

I finally started being an older sister to my younger siblings and it feels so great having that new type of bond with them. Before Lauren and Dani could drive, I would take them around to various places they needed to go. They really pushed me out of my insanely small driving comfort zone. They say hindsight is always twenty-twenty; looking back, it's insane how much time I wasted wanting to hang out with my older sisters while squandering opportunities to bond with my younger ones.

I realized as I got older that the isolation I felt was self-imposed. I spent so much time wishing I had the things I felt I lacked that I forgot to be grateful for what I did have. When we moved to LA, none of my siblings had any friends and we had to stick together. We became close out of necessity. We've cried, we've fought, we've opened up to one another. We became a tribe. I no longer feel stuck in the middle because stuck is a mindset! I see all the good things I can learn from every one of my siblings. I am grateful for my middle spot and I am so grateful for all of the lessons I've learned and the strength of our relationships!

Sisterly Advice

Lisa Cimorelli

I've learned a lot from my older siblings. My older brother Mike taught me how to be more open with people and how to take the initiative. Growing up, I always admired how outgoing he was. Whenever I'm feeling shy, I think, "What would Michael do?" My older sister Katherine has always been really in touch with her faith, and she inspired me to be more devout. But my oldest sister, Christina, played an even bigger role in shaping who I am today.

It started in 2009, before we all moved to LA. Christina would go to Barnes & Noble and read all these psychology books about family, how people interact, how your childhood affects you, how different things make you turn out different ways, and how to heal from them. Sometimes we'd just discuss things she read or she would point out things that she noticed about us, like patterns of behavior she'd seen and learned how to cope with. We would all talk about it.

When I was seventeen, she sat me down one day and said, "You never express your feelings. I have never heard you say, 'That hurt me, I'm upset.' But you have feelings; they are inside of you even though you ignore them and act like they don't exist. They do exist and you need to express them and let them out."

At first I was like, "No, what are you talking about? I don't do that." I'm really analytical and introverted so I form my own theories and process things very slowly. I didn't really want to see myself as some closed-off robot, but after thinking about it for a while I was like, *dang, she's right.*

I also got to feel the happiness, the joy, and the light again.

I knew I was sad and unhappy in my life; I always had this darkness and never really knew why. I learned from Christina that some things that happen to you can trigger old emotions. Because I had all those extra feelings bottled up inside, I was constantly trapped in my sadness, and if anything at all went wrong, I would just sink into it.

But I didn't understand the concept of saying it out loud and talking through it—it just seemed too painful—so Christina taught me about expressing myself through journaling. She told me to write, "*This* happened and it made me feel *this*," and to go back through my old memories and identify my feelings. That was a huge turning point for me. At first I thought, *Christina is crazy for telling me to do this, this is awful. I am so sad, I'm bawling my eyes out. How is this good? How does this help anything?*

But after several months of letting out all the sadness, I realized how much it helped. As I let go of the negative feelings, I started to write positive things in my journal. Even on bad days when I would start with *I feel fat, I feel ugly, I feel stupid, this person doesn't love me enough,* by the end it would turn into *I am beautiful, I am smart, this person wasn't being thoughtful but they do care about me.* As I started to feel everything for the first time—the anger, the guilt, the betrayal, the hurt, the sadness—I also got to feel the happiness, the joy, and the light again.

Now I am happy with who I am and I truly owe so much of that to Christina. She helped me so much in becoming the best version of myself, and I know in my heart I would not be the same person without my big sister. Not at all.

Sassy Is Not in My Nature

Katherine Cimorelli

I'm the third oldest in my family of eleven kids. Right above me is my sister Christina, who is eighteen months older than me, and below me is my sister Lisa, who is eighteen months younger. Growing up, it was like we were the three musketeers. As kids we spent hours outside, playing imaginative games where we were pioneers or fairies, making magic potions, and swinging on our swing set until the sun went down.

When I became a teenager, things changed drastically. I remember the painful feeling of insecurity creeping in around the age of thirteen. I started to compare myself to Christina and Lisa. Christina has this fiery, intense personality. I remember watching and being mystified—how did she always come across so charming and playful? Lisa, on the other hand, is wackier and more bizarre, but she seemed to have mastered witty banter—especially with boys.

I tried to be "sassy" like them, but it didn't feel genuine; it simply wasn't in my nature. At the time, I remember thinking that something was wrong with me. I remember walking up to a circle of kids my age and feeling overlooked and invisible, like I didn't add anything to the group and no one noticed me. The feeling crushed me.

By the time I was sixteen, I had almost no confidence in myself. I decided that it was beyond not being "sassy" enough—I thought it had to be my looks. I thought that was the reason that I felt so invisible and my sisters stood out. I would look in the mirror and pick out all my "flaws," wishing I were different.

The summer after I turned sixteen, something in me snapped. "Enough!" a voice inside of me said. It was too painful to be so insecure; out of necessity, something had to change. I knew there was only one choice—I had to find myself. Or, at least, I had to start looking.

I started at the library below my house. My family lived on top of a hill, and at the bottom was a big, beautiful library. I set a goal for myself to read a bunch of books that summer. I would walk up and down the hill and fill my backpack with books. My mind started expanding. I thought, *There are so many other people in this world, so many great stories—so much magic all around me. I've been missing it all along.*

Rather than trying to be like everyone else, I started exploring my own interests. I started skateboarding around my neighborhood with my little sister Lauren. It felt freeing and relaxing, cruising down those hills. I also started playing the bass guitar on summer nights, sitting on my front porch step, looking out at the swaying trees and singing along to songs by Forever the Sickest Kids and Stevie Wonder. I also found a new hobby that became one of the greatest tools of my life; I started writing.

Sitting on the rug in my room, scribbling by the dim light of my closet, I began pouring my heart out onto page after page, which I would fold up and put into a giant pink box under my bed. I kept everything. My hands throbbed and turned gray, covered in pencil lead, but my heart felt lighter and I felt like I could breathe again.

The greatest gift during this whole period of intense self-discovery (which, now that I am twenty-four, is still an exciting, ongoing process) was that, especially through writing and reading, I started to know myself, and I started to love myself. I was still the same person; I just shifted my focus. Instead of focusing on insecurity and what I didn't have, I started searching everywhere for beauty.

Now that I'm older, I see so much beauty in my sisters—the greatest beauty being how different we all are, and how we celebrate and embrace those differences. My prayer for you reading this is that you will see your own unique beauty, and embrace yourself. You deserve nothing less.

An Imperfect Role Model

Christina Cimorelli

I always thought being a role model meant you had to be perfect. In my family of eleven, I have one older brother, but I'm the oldest of the girls. And being the oldest, you feel like you have to be a role model in every single way because you go through everything first. Your sisters look to you in every category, so it sets you up from a very young age to be their go-to. I took that responsibility to mean that I needed to make sure I was doing my best in every aspect of my life; it just became my natural role from childhood.

In some of the categories, like braces, it was easy for me to be like, "I got my braces first, let me tell you all about it." But other categories were harder. I felt like I couldn't be very personal because if I told them I didn't do things perfectly, they would see it as a failure or a weakness.

Like in relationships, they would ask me how my boyfriend and I were doing, and I would

I stopped pretending to be perfect.

just want to say "great," or only mention good things and not mention anything we were struggling with. But the truth is all girlfriends and boyfriends have disagreements; it's an inevitable by-product of two people dating who are individuals—you're not always going to see eye to eye. But when my boyfriend and I would have a fight, I would want to keep it private and not show my siblings that I had any faults or flaws in that area. I thought, *I'm the oldest one; I should have a perfect relationship.*

Then one day I stopped pretending to be perfect. It was kind of an accident. I had a really big problem with my boyfriend, a conflict in our relationship, and I realized I needed to make some life changes to grow more as a person. My sisters are around me all the time, and they were going to notice that things were different, so I had to tell them.

I had planned out what I thought I was going to say. I was going to keep it vague—"So here's a little problem, I just need your help"—but I was going to minimize it. But as I started talking, I found myself spilling the whole truth; before I knew what was happening, it was just all coming out, all the details, and I didn't even know why.

In that moment, it was shocking and painful to be that vulnerable. I felt shame, guilt, failure, and fear. Even as I was talking, I thought, *Why am I doing this? What am I saying? They are never going to look up to me again.* It felt very dramatic, like in that instant I was giving up my position as role model and leader. It was very hard to finally feel seen and to not be hiding anymore. There was a part of admitting everything that felt good, but I was worried everyone would see me differently.

But instead of judgment, or disappointment in me, their immediate reaction was relief. There may have been a little disappointment, but it was mostly support and ultimately admiration for the way I could open up and be so honest. They told me they admired me for being vulnerable. They didn't see it as a *weakness*. They saw it as *brave*. I learned that they never wanted me to be flawless. They wanted to hear my struggles so they could learn from them. It was one of the hardest moments of my life, showing them my whole self, but in the end I'm glad I did it because they found strength in it—and so did I.

I learned that being a role model is not about being flawless and being perfect. It's not just succeeding. It's not about you putting on a mask. It's not really even about you. Being a role model is about being brave and putting yourself out there even when you're struggling. It's about showing people that when they're down they can get back up, just like you're getting up from hard times. Being a role model is about helping people get to their best place in life. And you can't help them get to that place of strength if they can't relate to you, and they can't relate if you're not being honest, if you're not being vulnerable. It's that vulnerability that you can connect to others. I am a better role model to my sisters now that I can admit I'm imperfect.

My Not-So-Sweet Sixteen

When I was sixteen years old, I had two things on my mind. The first one being getting a car, and the second one was, well . . . I was a sixteen-year-old boy, what do you think?

Speaking of, one day I was at my then-girlfriend's house when I got a text from my mom saying, *We're on our way to pick you up. And we have a big surprise!* I immediately knew that that big surprise was: My. First. Car. Hopefully a BMW, but honestly any German car would do. Since my birthday weeks before, I had been talking to my parents nonstop about it. It was going to be my way to freedom, my chance at exploration, and most important, my means of travel to Chipotle on a daily basis.

I put the phone down and told my girlfriend to put a jacket on, we were about to go for a drive in my new car. But as we walked outside, I noticed that only our usual family truck was waiting for us. The family truck definitely wasn't an Audi, I thought, but I'd take it.

That's when my mom got out of the car holding the actual surprise. It didn't have a turbo engine, heated seats, or a sunroof. My mom handed me . . . an actual baby, and it wasn't even named Mercedes.

Instead, his name was Kyle and he was my blond-haired, blue-eyed one-year-old nephew. He was my stepbrother's son, and since he and Kyle's mom weren't able to take care of him at the moment, we got to. For the entire drive home, Kyle looked at me from his car seat with his mouth wide open, drool pouring out of both sides. Honestly, I would've taken a used brown Volkswagen Bug at that point.

From that point on, I was more than an uncle. Most uncles you see only on Christmas or when he's asking your mom for a loan. Instead, I was a live-in uncle who was now expected to not only acknowledge this lump of a person, but also to play with it, feed it, and sometimes even clean its poop. Which, I don't know if it's just him or every baby, but he pooped all the time. I think the only time he stopped pooping was to pee.

The first time I was asked to watch him, I thought it would be easy. According to Louis CK (who provided me with all my child-rearing knowledge) there's just one rule: *Do not let him die.* So I thought my parents would leave, he'd sit in that bouncy chair thing, and I'd play video games for a couple of hours until they got back, and then boom, night over with no issues. I was wrong.

As soon as the door shut behind my parents, Kyle launched into a full-on nuclear-warning sob session. So I did what I had to do. I picked him up and ran outside to give him back to my parents. Unfortunately, they were already gone.

I proceeded to offer him every type of food we had, but nothing. I gave him his toys, my brother's toys, even MY toys, but nothing. I checked his diaper. Butt everything.

Even after I changed his diaper, though (because apparently they can't do it on their own), he kept crying. I couldn't think of what to do next, and I felt incapable. I felt like this little guy, who had done nothing wrong, was crying because of me. So out of desperation, I picked him up and held him in my arms so that our chests were touching, and I felt his painful screams start to quiet. They eventually became serene breathing, and after an hour of terror, of me just trying my hardest to make him smile, the little guy actually fell asleep in my arms.

Unfortunately, they were the same arms I wanted to play *Halo* with, but trying to set him down was like playing *Operation*, except it was rigged and you'd lose every time. So I didn't eat anything, didn't play anything, didn't do anything. I just held him.

When my parents came home I woke up and told them what happened, then asked for some sort of payment for my services. *He's alive, I did my job.* That's when they told me that he was family, and you don't get paid for watching family. And *that's when I* realized that being a parent is like babysitting for free for the rest of your life.

Kyle and I ended up becoming really close over the next few years. Then his parents came back into the picture and I became a regular uncle. I saw him more than twice a year, but I didn't have to wipe his butt anymore. And although my time as a temporary parent was short, it taught me one very important thing: I am not ready to be a parent.

I am not ready to do what my parents did for me. I am not ready to give up on almost all social occasions with friends. I am not ready to wake up four times a night to check on something that should be sleeping. And I definitely am not ready to be okay with getting someone else's poop on my finger accidentally. Yes, that happened to me, and it will happen to you.

Until I am ready for a baby, I'll just stick with a car. At least the car only needs to get its oil changed once every ten thousand miles.

FRIENDSHIP
FAMILY LOVE
③ SCHOOL
HEARTBREAK
Hustles
INSECURITIES
STRUGGLES

I'm looking through old yearbooks rn and my hair was on point. I know this is a throwback, but what's your favorite moment from school??

Aspyn Ovard Every sports game because I got to cheer. I love cheering! C-H-E-E-R-I-N-G!

Lauren Elizabeth When I finally quit cheerleading. I ended up going for the school musical and landed the role of dance captain.

Rebecca Black Same! My first audition ever was for the musical theater class. I sang Journey's "Don't Stop Believin'." At first I was terrified, but then I remember being like, "Oh, I can actually do this."

Meg DeAngelis Theater for me too!! We did *A Midsummer Night's Dream* and I finally felt like I was in my comfort zone.

Maddy Whitby I was president of my class every year. I won every election with the slogan "Vote for Maddy, You'll Be Gladdy."

That might be the best slogan ever. 👏

Alex Aiono One time I did a math problem in my head that my math teacher didn't think I could do. IN YOUR FACE!! IT'S FOUR!

Ryan Abe At a pep rally my friends and I did a choreographed dance to "I Want It That Way" by the Backstreet Boys. I air-humped my principal.

Claudia Sulewski Senior prom! Getting to see everyone one last time before moving away meant so much to me.

Andrew Lowe Graduating.

I'm with you, man. 🎉

What was your favorite moment in school?
Tweet me @HunterMarch with #TBHMyFavoriteMomentInSchool

The Worst Thing I Did in School. According to Everyone.

In school, I didn't get in **that** much trouble . . . mostly because I was afraid of my mom. But I did have a couple of run-ins with faculty that I could've and should've avoided. For example, after I found out my middle school principal's full name, our next interaction began with "What's good, Susan?" For the rest of the day, nothing was *good* for me.

Another day, when a substitute came in, I decided to pretend I was absent and answer roll call as one of my friends, who actually **was** absent. After I moved the substitute's printer to the other side of the room **three** times, my friend's parents were called in for a disciplinary meeting with me. *Hi, Mom? Hi, Dad?* Let's just say everyone was confused.

But those usually only led to long conversations about my actions, which led to an apology from me, and nothing more. I thought *nothing bad could happen, it's only school.* Then I got caught cheating on a math test and all of a sudden, my whole word was flipped upside down.

Apparently "studying" is supposed to prepare you for "tests." Problem was, I wasn't studying anything besides Rainbow Road on *Mario Kart*. What up, Yoshi. Every once in a while I would do well on a test. Through deductive reasoning and a little luck, I could pull through with a B, or even an A. Other times, I would bubble in (C) all the way to the end and pray that this was **the test** where that actually worked. It never was. I now (C) that.

This all came to a head, though, when I arrived remarkably unprepared for a trigonometry test. The problem with trigonometry is that there really is no deductive reasoning, and when you have to show your work, there is zero luck involved. I knew that this test was going to be a bad one. I accepted that and was ready to take it, fail it, and hide the evidence from my mother. But then, right before the test was given out, a classmate handed me the answers. It was a copy of the test from an earlier period, and it looked like it was completed by Pythagoras himself. It was flawless, it was beautiful, and it was now in my hands. A number of kids in the class had copied and passed it on, and I was last to get it. With no time to copy, I just hid it under my desk.

Should I become . . . a cheater?

But should I use this literal cheat sheet? Is it morally right to take credit for someone else's work? Someone who spent hours upon hours becoming the student who I wished I could be? Should I become . . . a cheater?

One hundred percent yes. I'm sorry, but you don't know what it's like to have *my mom* yell at you. I copied every number and equation off that test with precision. I finished; my plan worked. Then I got cocky, turned the test in first, and asked the teacher if she wanted me to work on anything else while the rest of the class finished.

At that point, she knew that I did not know what *X* was in any of these equations. With suspicion, she asked to see what was under my desk. I told her that under my desk were the incredible notes I took because she was just a phenomenal teacher who made tests like this easy. She still wanted to look under my desk, and she found it. Everyone was looking at me, and I was looking at the floor. Even I couldn't think of a joke to get me out of this one. She took me straight to the principal's office and my parents were called. It only got worse from there.

They were throwing around words like *suspension, permanent record,* even *expulsion.* That was when I learned that there was a zero-tolerance policy for cheating in my school . . . Ah, whatever, who am I trying to kid? I always knew there was a zero-tolerance cheating policy, I just didn't think I would get caught.

The final punishment was a fail on the test, and being removed from both of my extracurricular activities. One was the varsity soccer team, and the other was academic decathlon. (I know what you're thinking: What was a cheater like me doing on academic decathlon? Well, I did the speech portion of it, because all I did was talk in class anyway.) Then, after I may or *may not* have cried, they lowered the punishment to being removed from only one of those two teams, at my choosing. Academic decathlon had ended and I had already given my speech; they hadn't selected the medalists yet, but it was basically over. Meanwhile, my soccer team was in the play-offs and the guys were counting on me (to warm up the bench) so it seemed like an easy choice.

Aside from my mother's wrath, and the failing grade on the test (which would've happened anyway), I thought I had gotten off easy. I even thought that I had kind of won. Then came the first hit of reality. My academic decathlon teacher told me that I won the gold medal in speech, but I wouldn't get the medal because I had been removed from the team. I had spent months working on that speech, countless nights reading it aloud to family members and classmates for their notes, all for nothing. Then came the second hit: Our soccer team was eliminated in the first play-off game, which was just like a big kick in the . . . soccer balls.

I was disappointed with myself for even considering cheating in the first place. I was ashamed for abandoning my academic decathlon team. And I was embarrassed when I realized that everyone in my classes knew me as the *cheater*.

And it was all because I decided to cheat on that one test. Listen, I know how pointless we all think trigonometry is. At the time I thought it was stupid, but as I've learned since that horrible day, it turns out that there are actually a lot of not-horrible careers that use trigonometry. Navigators use trigonometry to make sure my plane doesn't hit your plane in the sky, which is awesome. Astronauts use it to get into space. Radiologists, economists, computer engineers, nuclear engineers, basically all engineers use trigonometry. That includes my personal favorite, game engineers. Like the ones who made *Mario Kart*. They used trigonometry on a game that made me not study trigonometry. The irony.

I may have cheated on a test, but more so I cheated myself out of a gold medal and a month of freedom. Most important, though, I cheated myself out of the chance to be an engineer on the best video game ever created, *Mario Kart*.

SIX THINGS I LOVED ABOUT MIDDLE SCHOOL . . .

1. _____

2. _____

3. _____

4. _____

5. _____

6. _____

(I didn't love anything about middle school.)

First Day of College: Expectation vs. Reality

Vanessa Merrell

When I started college I hadn't even been in an actual classroom since halfway through my sophomore year, when my family moved to California. Both my sister and I loved school. We were very busy students. We got straight As, we were in advanced classes, on the honor roll, in broadcasting, theater, and choir—basically all the things. When we moved to California, we went to an independent school, like home school, so we could pursue YouTube and acting, but there weren't advanced classes or extracurriculars so it wasn't really the same. So for college I was really excited to meet actual students and, more important, to get a real teacher and to actually get to learn from someone and not just teach myself. I had a lot of expectations of what college would be like, but college is nothing like I expected.

From left to right: Veronica, Vanessa

CLASSES

Expectations:

College classes would be just like high school classes but, like, ten times harder.

Reality:

College classes are definitely harder, but they are NOTHING like high school classes. In college you get to learn so many things and you get to pick what you learn. Sure, there are electives in high school, but in college you have, like, a million options to choose from. I'm majoring in television and film production, so I am learning a lot that will help me for my future, but I'm also just expanding my horizons. Like, I took a sociology class to learn about the way people make decisions and why they are the way they are.

TEACHERS

Expectations:

In the movies, college professors are either, like, old guys who rap or old guys who put you to sleep. But either way they are old guys (usually with those weird elbow patches on brown plaid blazers).

Reality:

In my first class, English, this guy who was about 5'3" and looked my age walked to the front of the classroom and said "Welcome to college, I'm your professor," and told us he would be teaching the class. I laughed because I thought it was a joke. I thought he was a student in my class pretending to be my professor. But SURPRISE, he really was my teacher! He was a TA, which means he was a graduate student who also teaches classes. He was on our level and he was not afraid to be himself.

Another professor was this 6'1" tall, skinny woman. She was very intense, very standoff-ish—like the kind of professor who would just show up to class, teach, and leave. But in a totally unexpected way, she ended up being one of my favorite professors. Since I have to travel a lot for work, I had to e-mail her and talk to her to know what I was going to miss. She was really helpful; she would give me extra-credit opportunities. She would ask me questions about my career and I got to know her on a personal level. When you have a personal connection with the professor, it makes class easier, even when it's a tough professor like her.

FITTING IN

Expectations:

In high school there was pressure to wear certain clothes, do your hair a certain way, act a certain way, listen to certain songs, watch certain popular movies. I was totally prepared to face the same pressure in college with a whole new list of things that were cool.

Reality:

In college there is ZERO pressure to be any one way. The students are diverse in every way. Some people dress very formally. Some girls even wear heels. There are some girls completely bumming in their pajamas and guys who don't even shower. And there's also everything in between. There isn't one band, or one movie, or one way to act. More than that, people think it's cool to be friends with people who like different stuff because it means you can learn new things from your friends! It isn't just one thing.

MAKING FRIENDS

Expectations:

Making friends in college is super easy because college is basically a nonstop party, right?

Reality:

Even though there's no pressure to be any one way, making friends was still a lot harder than I thought. When I arrived at my first class on my first day (after what was basically a scavenger hunt to find my classroom because I had gone to entirely the wrong building) there was only one guy sitting there. After the quick relief of *phew, I'm not late*, I sat right down next to him. Another eight students walked in and they all sat kind of separate from one another. Everyone was VERY quiet. I thought, *College is a place to make new friends; why is no one talking to anyone else?*

FREEDOM

Expectations:

I'm free! I'm FREEEEEEEE!

Reality:

There is DEFINITELY a lot of freedom in college. You can set your own schedule. You can stay up as late as you want. You don't really have homework. There are tons of fun things going on basically every night of the week. But with that freedom comes A LOT of responsibility.

On my first day of college, my tough professor said, "All right, you show up or you don't; I don't take attendance, but we're going to have an exam next week." So they really put the choice on you. You can totally skip class without getting in trouble, but things move fast in college, so missing one day is like missing a whole week in high school! I know people who didn't go and they failed. And even though you don't have homework, you have papers, exams, and more reading than you have ever had in your life. And that's coming from some-one who LOVES to read. My best advice is don't procrastinate and be organized—very, very organized.

I know a lot of YouTubers don't go to college, but for me and my sister, it was really important. It was just one of the values we grew up with. You go to school, then you go to college. That mindset isn't necessarily the same with everyone. I think it's important to educate your-self. But I think the biggest lesson I learned this year is that college is definitely not what I expected—it's better.

First Day Anxiety

Veronica Merrell

For some reason, I have no problem speaking on camera. I'm comfortable and free to be me. However, I was incredibly nervous on my first day of college. I was no longer in my room speaking confidently on camera. Going to a class full of people I've never talked to was nerve-racking, and all I wanted to do was make a good first impression.

It's weird. If I have a scheduled presentation in class, I can knock it out with no problem. But if a teacher calls on me out of the blue, *my mind goes into complete anxiety overload.* I panic and think, *What if I say the wrong thing; what if they think I'm dumb?* Being a person who struggles with social anxiety, I almost literally left and went home on the first day. But I didn't ditch! I couldn't! Because honestly, it would have given me even worse anxiety!

From left to right: Veronica, Vanessa

I like to think of myself as a good student. Not only would I never ditch, I actually love to sit in the front row. For some reason I figured that I would be left alone there, so I picked a front seat way in the corner. I was wrong.

When my Urban Studies class began, the professor said, "Hello, guys. Time to introduce yourselves!" and then he looked straight at me. I thought, *Great, I have to talk first in front of everyone.*

Then, in my second class, Central American Writing, IT HAPPENED AGAIN. Maybe this front-row tactic thing wasn't a good idea. The teacher asked us to write down our names, our favorite artists, our favorite movie, or what we like to do for fun. After we were all done

My college experience looked nothing like my high school . . .

writing down our answers, she asked us to read them aloud and OF COURSE started with me.

Now, my favorite artist is "Banana Pancakes" singer Jack Johnson, but as you all know, there is also a Viner named Jack Johnson. I thought, *What a great time to make a little joke.* So I said, "I'm Veronica Merrell. I like X and my favorite artist is Jack Johnson . . . and I don't mean the Viner," then giggled. No one laughed. Not one person. It was AWKWARD. And for the rest of class that day, that moment was playing over and over again in my head.

I dropped it and later went on to talk about how I love to watch YouTube. That didn't work either. In fact, no one in the class seemed to be a part of social media; I mean, they weren't even on Twitter. It was a weird thing for me because I'm a YouTuber, and my life revolves around social media. On the other hand, it was pretty much a relief. Yes, I'm very proud of my YouTube channel, but sometimes people treat me differently when they find out. In that classroom, I felt . . . normal.

My college experience looked nothing like my high school in Kansas City. I grew up in a predominantly white community. Some people at my school were really small-minded about people from other cultures. My dad is English and German and my mom is Spanish and Portuguese. I got made fun of for being of some Latin descent.

But in college there are people of all different religions, ethnicities, and backgrounds. And my Central American Writing class had a lot of people of Latin descent like me, which was an incredible feeling. I finally had stuff in common with peers that I never had in high school. Their mom makes them clean every Saturday too!

Having similarities can be important to help you feel comfortable at first, but it's also important to learn from people who are different from you. I was learning that though being a clone was important in high school, being yourself was ideal in college. If you're in high school right now, just hold tight a little longer . . . people will appreciate your weirdly specific humor in college. I promise.

I mean, yes, I still get nervous in class sometimes, but I don't have to worry about being judged. I'll still crack jokes even if I know people won't laugh. At some point you have to accept that you are who you are, funny or not so much, and that's okay. Somehow, it makes me a little less nervous to be a little more me.

CLASSES THEY SHOULD TEACH IN HIGH SCHOOL BUT DON'T

SCHEDULE

1. Taxes 101:
Why You Make Less Than You Think You Do

2. Introduction to Laundry:
How One Red Sock Can Ruin Everything

3. Plumbing, Elective:
Because There Are Some Things You Shouldn't Fix Yourself

4. E-mailing in the Workplace:
Stop Putting 69 In Your E-mail Address

5. Advanced Language:
Words Never to Use Around Adults, Like *Fleek*

6. Spare Keys 1B:
It's Cheaper to Call a Friend Than a Locksmith

7. The Art of Grocery Shopping:
You Can Have Too Many Eggs

8. Fundamentals of Fridge Cleaning:
Really, You Can Have Too Many Eggs

9. Cooking on a Budget:
All the Uses of Cereal

10. Manners:
Please Take This Class, Thank You

I'm Not Worthless

Aija Mayrock

Halloween my freshman year in high school was the scariest day of my life. But it wasn't scary because of a ghost or a monster—it was scary because in one moment, my life turned upside down.

Just a year before, I had moved from New York to California. While in New York, I had been relentlessly bullied. And when I moved to California and started a new life, it seemed like a giant Band-Aid had "fixed" the problem. I made new friends, I started acting in plays and writing stories, and the bullying had stopped.

Halloween that year started like every other Halloween. I dressed up, had a great day at school, ate way too much candy, and laughed with some friends. But then it all changed.

I got a text message from a classmate I had known in New York. The text included a photo of a girl I didn't know wearing a big sign around her neck. The sign had my name on it: Aija

Mayrock. I was so confused. Who was this person? I went on Facebook and saw dozens of people posting the same picture. A girl whom I'd never met dressed up as "me" for Halloween.

I started scavenging through Facebook and found many people posting the same picture. There were hundreds of comments per picture, with people writing variations of the following comments:

"Aija should kill herself. No one wants her alive." "No one likes her. No one would care if she died." "Her face makes me want to vomit."

As I read these comments, I froze in a complete state of shock. But the strangest part was that more than half of these people were strangers to me. I had never met or heard of them. So why did they all hate me so much?

I had never been so afraid of the world.

I messaged the girl who dressed up as me. Let's call her Sara. I wrote, "I don't know who you are or why you are doing this, but why would you dress up as me for Halloween?"

Instead of apologizing or even ignoring me, she posted an image of my note to her on Facebook, which only garnered even MORE attention and even MORE brutal comments threatening to kill me and urging me to take my own life. Each post hit my heart like a dagger.

I had been impersonated and humiliated three thousand miles away by a girl I didn't even know and the Band-Aid had been ripped off my new life in California.

I had never been so afraid of the world. I had never felt so alone, so hated, and so lost.

That day I went home and told my mom everything. We found Sara's home number and spoke to her mom. When Sara got on the phone and apologized, I finally felt a wave of relief.

But a few days later, I got a message from Sara saying, "I'm not done. I will never be done." Within hours, my phone began to ring nonstop. I would get fifty phone calls a day from blocked numbers. If I picked up, people would brutally bully me, laugh, or just hang up.

I felt like everyone in the world hated me. It seemed like everyone wanted me gone. There was no escape from the flood of messages, posts, comments, and phone calls.

I didn't know how much more I could handle before I just broke. So I deleted all of my social media accounts and changed my phone number.

Suddenly, there was quiet. That's when my thoughts started to haunt me. Although I was off social media, my mind suddenly became my worst bully. I would hear the words, the comments, and everything that my bullies said on repeat in my mind. I felt completely worthless.

I started to wear baggy clothes to hide my body. I picked at my food and lost fifteen pounds in a matter of weeks. I never left the house except to go to school. I began to avoid people.

Maybe if I was invisible, no one would be mean to me?

Luckily, a few weeks later, my life changed forever. I saw a poster at my school for a film festival that was accepting screenplays. It was the day of the deadline. I had always loved writing and so I rushed home and wrote my very first screenplay, about bullying. It was the first time I confronted my feelings about being bullied. As I began to write, tears streamed down my face. I didn't even know that I was crying. I couldn't stop typing, and the stories, memories, and forgotten moments of my past flooded me. I had built a wall around myself to protect me from bullying, but in that moment, that wall was torn down. I realized that my feelings were valid. It was okay that I felt sad, scared, fragile, and alone. I had a purpose on this planet and an important story to tell. I had been told I was "worthless" by my peers time and time again, but as I began to write about my past, I realized that I AM NOT WORTHLESS.

A week later, I was notified that my screenplay was accepted and was going to be made into a film. Three months after the film was produced, I won "best screenplay" in the film festival.

As I stood on that stage, I realized the power of creativity. I was able to channel all of my pain and fear into a film—something that many others could watch and relate to.

From that moment forward, I decided that I would dedicate my life to giving a voice to the voiceless. And that's when I started writing my book, *The Survival Guide to Bullying.* My mission was to create a book that would help millions of kids around the world survive bullying. A few months after it came out in the United States and in thirteen foreign countries, I began to receive hundreds of thousands of messages every day from kids around the world saying things like, "Your book saved my life. I didn't know if I could keep going on, but your story has shown me that I can survive."

It's not easy for me to share my story with the world. It's scary to be brave and have a voice. But I also feel a duty to share this story with you and every other person being bullied. You are NOT ALONE. There is NOTHING WRONG WITH YOU. I know this because I have felt that way for too many years. Bullying won't last forever.

And always remember this: In those moments when you feel that there is no hope, remember that I have had those moments too. And so has every other person who has been bullied. But we have the power to move past our difficulties. We have the ability to change our lives. I have done it and I know that you can too.

GUYS! It's my anniversary this week and I want to make sure I don't mess this night up. What's the most memorable date you've been on?? Good or bad!

Aija Mayrock This guy and I were at dinner and in the middle of our meal, he pulled out the mask from *Phantom of the Opera* and started to serenade me in front of the whole restaurant . . .

Wait, is that good or . . . 😖

Alex Aiono I spent the whole day at Disneyland with a girl!! It's such a sick date because spending that much time together lets you really learn a lot about someone. Like . . . how they deal with long lines and the whole churro or no churro dilemma.

Claudia Sulewski One day? Try four. My most memorable date was definitely taking a trip to attend his sister's wedding. Does a four-day trip count as a first date??

Andrew Lowe Seventh grade at the Cheesecake Factory with my girlfriend at the time. We were like waiting for our parents to pick us up. She closed her eyes and puckered her lips, so I kissed her. Then she said she was just kidding.

That's the weirdest/best "just kidding" ever.

Maddy Whitby I was on this great date . . . then I walked out of the bathroom and the guy was like, "Um, you've got toilet paper stuck to your foot." I laughed and thought, *Wow, this guy has jokes.* But it was SUPER true. I had a comically long piece of toilet paper stuck to my shoe.

Aspyn Ovard When my husband proposed. That was a good one.

Okay, Aspyn, you win. 👏

Have a memorable date?
Tweet me @HunterMarch with #TBHMyMostMemorableDate

The Art of Flirting
How Much Does A Polar Bear Weigh?

Enough to break the ice. Hi, I'm Hunter. You know how I said in the introduction of this book that I used to think yelling at girls across the playground was a good way to flirt with them? Well, in case I wasn't clear, it is *not* a good way. In fact, most people don't like that at all. It is a good way, though, to make sure people think you're insane . . . so if that's what you're going for, awesome. Ya nailed it!

The reason I did that, though, is because I didn't *know* any other way. It's hard! And when the hundredth person in a row says they "have a boyfriend," you start wondering if everyone magically started dating each other overnight. The problem is, there's no rule book for flirting. And if there were, it would be LONG, because flirting changes based on who you are, who the person you're flirting with is, the time, the place, the everything! It also depends heavily on the stage of the relationship. Flirting with someone you just met on a dating app is different from flirting with someone you've been dating for a few months.

But honestly, if you're at the "few months" stage, you're just fine with whatever you've been doing. So I'll just focus on the hardest part of dating: The Approach.

For me, it took years of trial and error, and error, and error just to get a few phone numbers, and honestly some of those were fake. One time, I bought a school lunch for a girl who I liked, which she rejected because, and I quote, "That looks gross." It was the most heart-breaking one dollar I've ever spent. Another time I simply asked a girl if she was ready to settle down with me. She wasn't; in fact, she never even told me her name.

Eventually, I learned some more effective flirting techniques that I'll share with you now:

USING THE FRIEND

Asking a friend of yours, or of your crush, to play a part in the flirting process is a beginner's favorite for a number of reasons. First, it takes a lot less confidence to tell a third party to do the dirty work of talking to your crush for you. Second, high school and middle school are PERFECT for this because odds are you have at least one mutual friend with them. And finally, if you get rejected, your friend always breaks the news to you in a nice way. Well, sometimes.

Whenever I started crushing on someone, I'd always ask classmates if they knew her. If one did, I would ask them to find out if she was single, if we had anything in common, if she had scary older brothers, etc. If the coast was clear, I'd ask a friend to go talk to the girl, and I would just so happen to join the conversation . . . you know, randomly.

The only problem with this is that without you talking to your crush *yourself*, they may not realize how great you are, or how beautiful your eyes are up close, and they may pass up the opportunity.

Personality best for this: Shy people. If approaching complete strangers is frightening, this is the way to go!

DID IT HURT? DID WHAT HURT? PICKUP LINES

As someone who loves to entertain, *pickup lines* were always one of my favorite ways to approach people. When I'd be out with my dad and brother, I would actually use *them* as a part of my pickup line. I'd approach my future girlfriend (confidence is key) and point to my dad and brother behind me, who'd usually wave, and I'd say, "I told them that I was going to approach you and they bet me twenty dollars that I would never get a phone number from someone that out of my league, and I agree it probably won't happen, but I like beating them, so if you wouldn't mind, can you just pretend and at least give me a fake phone number?" Then nine times out of ten, they'd write down their real phone number.

Now you may not go to that extreme, but just remember that a pickup line is supposed to be flattering and innocent. And even as a guy, I would find it flattering and unique to have a pickup line tried on me, so go for it! When done right, it's lighthearted, fun, and gets a laugh to start the conversation. When done wrong, it's overly aggressive, creepy, and gets a slap to end the conversation. It takes confidence to risk embarrassment like that, and a bit of comedic timing to pull off, but when done well, pickup lines can be a great icebreaker.

Personality best for this: Brave people! Think Superwoman, a fireman, or Jaden Smith. The risks involved are perfect for daredevils looking for that great story to tell their grandkids one day.

INSTAGRAM LIKE, LIKE, LIKE

This social media method is perfect for someone you *don't know* and have *zero mutual friends with*. I know about this technique personally, not because I've done it, but because my younger brother is the KING of it. He's mastered the formula, and, yes, there is a formula. Let me break it down. First, he likes two of her recent photos, because one isn't enough to get noticed. Once she likes a photo back, he likes a photo from a few weeks before. That's what lets her know that he's interested. If she does the same, he comments on her picture with the sunglasses emoji to start a conversation, because he's cool, and then he's only a couple of steps away from setting up a date with her.

Personality best for this: Adventurous people. You're doing this to someone you DON'T know, which is a big step out of the comfort zone, but it also opens up the dating pool. Who knows, you might end up dating my brother.

~~PLAY~~ BE HARD TO GET

"Play hard to get" has been one of the most common pieces of dating advice since the dawn of time. People will tell you to *wait a couple of days before texting back*, then when you do, *make it short, and always pretend you're busy!*

And while this *might* work, the problem is in the words themselves. "Playing" means games, which is NEVER the right thing. It creates confusion and distrust in any potential relationship. So to avoid that, you should instead BE hard to get. Use the time you would spend *playing* and instead play a sport, hang out with your friends, or study something you actually care about, and just generally be *actually busy*. When you do this, you'll also notice that your standards go way up because you don't have time for people who aren't worth yours.

Personality best for this: Anxious people. This is the best way to not only come off appealing, but also to distract yourself during the stressful times of *OMG, why haven't they texted me?*

THE BEST WAY

When I was younger, I tried every one of the flirting techniques I mentioned above . . . and some that were so bad they didn't even make the list, but after all that experimenting, I managed to find the perfect one. It **guarantees** that your crush will not only notice you, but that they'll *talk* to you. You ready? Okay, here it is. Next time you see them, walk right up to them and say . . . *hi*. That's it. I know, it sounds awful and you want to shut this book, but I promise that you'll *want* to try it!

For me it's always easier when I change my goal. When I'm planning on talking to my crush, my goal isn't to get a phone number or set up a date, my goal is to just *say* something to them. Simple as that. *Just speak words*. I can only control what I say to them, not what they do or say in return, so why would I worry about that? If I manage to say hello to them, regardless of what happens next, I've succeeded, and anything afterward is just icing on the cake.

It also helps to have a plan. The hardest part was always starting the conversation, because everything I'd want to say sounded awkward in my mind. So eventually I learned to keep it simple, and I would start with a "Hi, how are you?" or a "Are you in Ms. So-and-So's class?" Then after I got comfortable with that, I started including compliments in my first lines, which always catches someone's attention. "Excuse me, but I really like your jacket" almost guarantees that someone has to respond with a "Thank you." That exchange might become a conversation, which may lead to something more.

Personality type for this: *ALL OF THEM.* This is the most tried-and-true way of starting a conversation with the person you like. It's by far my favorite because I always accomplish my goal of just saying hi. By the way, hi. I like the way you read.

BEGINNER'S GUIDE TO FLIRTING WITH EMOJIS

Emojis are the newest and simplest way to flirt. But if you use the wrong one, you could be sending the wrong, really awkward message. So let me help you avoid a moment with this Beginner's Guide to Flirting with Emojis:

 The classic flirt. Always a good choice when you want to let someone casually know that you're interested in them. It can also be used if you're happy that you have something in your eye.

 The blushing face simply means *you make me smile*. Even though technically a regular smiley face also means *you make me smile*. THIS IS FOR YOUR CRUSH. They deserve their own blushing smiley face.

 You're hot . . . Or *it's getting hot in here . . .* Or *your latest mixtape is flames.*

 Any food emoji followed by a "?" and you've asked someone out on a date without using any words! Perfect for when you're totally ready to take the relationship out into the world, but not totally ready to risk getting rejected out in the real world. Also great if you're too hungry to type out "Chipotle?"

or These mean exactly what you think: *kiss time*. And both of these are totally great flirting emojis for AFTER YOU'VE ACTUALLY KISSED THAT PERSON. Do it too early and you might scare someone off, so once you've locked lips IRL, you're good to go. Oh, and never send because no one kisses with their eyes open. That's weird.

 Contrary to popular belief, this is a great flirting emoji. It says *You're annoying, but I like that.*

 I'm fun.

 I'm insane.

 I'm sorry for whatever I did (even if I don't know what I did). If that doesn't work, though ↓

 I'm *really* sorry for whatever *I* did.

 You leave me speechless. I personally have never used it, because I don't think I've ever run out of things to say, but you totally should! It's low risk and a great way to let your crush know you think they're special.

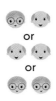 *I really like whatever you just said.*

 I want to grow old with you. This one is best left for when you've been in a relationship with someone for a really long time. And if you're going to send this one, you better at least be Facebook official.

or

or

and . . .

$%*# just got real.

What emojis do you use to flirt?
Tweet me at @HunterMarch with #TBHMyFlirtingEmoji

What NOT to Do During Your First Kiss

I hope you're ready to feel awkward, because I'm about to make it awkward. Let's talk about my first kiss. Looking back on it, it was horrible and awful and I'm sorry to everyone who took part. In the moment, though, *it was awesome.*

I had my first kiss in the summer after ninth grade, which, among my friends (and my little brother) made me a late bloomer. Anyway, I had been flirting with this girl "Rachel" via AOL Instant Messenger and things were getting pretty hot. I'm talking all types of pre-emoji emojis. ;) So we decided that my brother's upcoming middle school graduation would be the place where we would meet again. And I decided that I was going to kiss her . . . or at least try.

The day finally came. As I watched my brother don his graduation gown, pull the tassel back, and strike a pose for my proud mother, I thought to myself, *Should I use tongue?* That's when I got a text from Rachel that read, *Here.* And suddenly that word became one of the most exciting words in the English language. Right up there with "free Wi-Fi" and "unlimited soup, salad, and breadsticks." I wished my brother good luck, or didn't, whatever, and went off to meet the *love of my day* in the back of the school where we could be alone.

And as cool as all of this was for me, in all honesty, I was terrified. On my way to find her, my heart was racing faster than I was and my palms were drenched. That's when I decided we were NOT going to hold hands during this kiss and I would not grab her face. But then I thought, *Where in the world do I put my hands?! My pockets? HER pockets? Whoa. That's too far, Hunter.*

Anyway. I met her at the spot that will forever be the romantic home of my first kiss, by the double doors of the boys' locker room. #DreamWedding. She stood there, like a pro. And I stood there, pouring sweat like my hands were fire hydrants. So we talked about . . . I don't remember; it really does not matter. Then I decided, *This is it. This is the moment.* As she leaned on a wall, I dove in. I put my hands on the wall behind her. Our lips touched. That's when I realized: I never decided whether to use tongue. *GREAT! Now I'm sitting here gulping the air between our mouths, waiting to see if she does anything with her tongue. She doesn't. Should I do it? IT'S TOO LATE NOW, HUNTER!*

After about fifteen seconds of what I can only imagine was mediocre kissing for her, we stopped. I looked her in the eyes, my mouth still awkwardly open. Then, with no other option, I wrapped my arms around her shoulders and hugged her. *WHAT??? WHY WOULD YOU DO THAT?? GO BACK TO KISSING LIKE OUT-OF-BREATH FISH!*

Finally, we get back to kissing. *No tongue, but I feel like that's our thing now. No tongue. It's always been our thing, ever since we started kissing. We like to kiss as if we're sharing an invisible meatball. Delicious.* Back to the story.

The kissing started slowing down. She pulled her head back. Our eyes met. A spark flew.

And I went in for the . . . hug. *NOOOOOO!!! DIDN'T YOU LEARN THE FIRST TIME? Wait, hold on. Are we SWAYING BACK AND FORTH WHILE HUGGING?! GOOD-BYE CHANCES OF MAKING HER YOUR GIRLFRIEND NOW, WEIRDO! END THIS HUG IMMEDIATELY!*

We started kissing again, and then hugging, and then this kiss, hug cycle started and lasted for about, um, too long. And right as I was starting to question whether this whole kissing thing was for me, the kid who bullied me for all of middle school came around the corner with two of his oversize henchmen. He saw us as we were deep in the kiss part of the cycle and started hollering our names with some kissing noises. Rachel was mortified. She was blushing, and embarrassed, and just devastated that she had been exposed like that.

My mom called me right then to tell me I had to go watch my mood-killing little brother walk across the stage. So I left her there, my cheeks still flushed from embarrassment, and thought, *Someone saw me kissing. There's proof.*

I walked away from that moment with two key pieces of life advice: 1) I should never kiss someone like that again. 2) It took time, but I realized everybody's first kiss is awkward. It doesn't matter how old you are, or how many weeks you may or may not have been dating, your first kiss will be awkward. So instead of dreading every second of it, or looking back on it for years thinking you should've used tongue, just enjoy it. And realize that without a terrible first kiss, you'll never have a better second kiss.

P.S. My second kiss was also awkward. But my third was incredible. For me. She still thought it was weird. I've got to stop the hugging thing.

When Hunter Met ~~Sally~~ Lex

Not to brag or anything, but I have a girlfriend. I've had one for over three years now, and I have the YouTube videos to prove it. From our debut, "Girlfriend Tag!", to the time that she sobbed when I made her watch a sad commercial, people know about our lives (and her crying face). A lot of people have seen these videos and tweeted me asking how they can find someone just like I did. Someone to ride into the sunset with, a partner in crime! *(Or a partner in good if you're not into crime.)* But honestly, I don't know how it happened. I don't even know why she still likes me. I do know, though, that it all started with me doing her favorite thing: making her coffee.

My first job was as a Starbucks barista. Yep, green apron, black hat, health benefits. But I was seventeen years old, so the dental care didn't really excite me. The benefit I really cared about was all the women coming in for their upside-down Caramel Macchiatos. Then summer came around and it was all passion . . . tea. But fall was by far the best; nothing says

Like the croissants in our pastry case, nothing lasted.

spice like a Pumpkin Spice Latte. I met a few girls working there, but like the croissants in our pastry case, nothing lasted. That was, until Easter Sunday. That's when *she* walked in.

She was there with her mom and was towering over the other customers, and she had this dark hair that I'm pretty sure was made of 100 percent magic. I needed to speak to her. Problem was, I WASN'T WORKING THE REGISTER! I was on cleanup duty! So I waited for them to order their drinks, then when they separated I went up to her mom at the milk bar.

I said, "Excuse me, but your sister is gorgeous." *Nice job, Hunter.*

Her mom laughed and said that *she* wasn't her sister, that *she* was her daughter, and we started chatting. After finding out that my dream girl's name was Lex and that she was a UCLA student (smart girls FTW), I asked her mom if I could ask Lex out. Her mom said an enthusiastic, "Sure." So I set out. I nervously approached the prettiest girl I'd ever met, told her that I had her mom's blessing, and she gave me her phone number. HER REAL PHONE NUMBER. Believe me . . . I was as shocked as you are.

The day of the date I left home for my one-hour trek to Westwood at the peak of LA traffic, I was sweating in my gray Jetta, thinking simultaneously that this was the best and worst moment of my life thus far. She was way too beautiful for me, and the fact that she had set up an actual date with me was beyond my wildest dreams. When I finally made it, I found prime parking in front of the Coffee Bean where we had planned to meet. I know. Ironic.

I paced inside that Coffee Bean for about twenty minutes, wondering, *Should I order something for myself to look nonchalant, or wait for her and just order whatever she's getting?* This is how crazy men are. All of them. Then I got a text. It was from her. It read, *I'm not going to make it, I have to go do . . .* I don't remember much of the text after that, and I never ordered my drink. I walked back to my car and of course, I had a parking ticket. I ended up spending seventy-five dollars on a date I never had.

Why would I have ever thought I had a chance with this female superhero? She was too tall, too beautiful, too smart for me. Whatever; I moved on. I dated people, gained some confidence, and found my passion in making internet videos. One video in particular hit it big for me; it was called "Sh*t Valley Girls Say." In it, I dressed up as a Valley Girl and made fun of the, like, totally, like, awesome things, like, Valley Girls, say like, whatever, like. It became *valley* viral, meaning strangers would come up to me and say they'd seen my video, and that I looked good in a bikini. And at that point I realized making online videos was what I wanted to do. Not long after that I got a job at AwesomenessTV, and my life became everything I wanted it to be.

Then, three years after our first meeting, again on Easter Sunday, I get a text. It was from *Lex . . .* And all I could think as I read that name was, *Who is Lex?* THREE YEARS HAD GONE BY!

The name was saved, but I had NO idea who this person was, so I decided to play it cool. I called her to see if I could recognize the voice . . .

Nope. That didn't work. So not very smoothly I asked a series of weird questions to try to figure out who she was, ending with an ask to FaceTime (so I could see her face); then Lex said, "You don't know who this is, do you?" She caught me. She then reminded me who she was, and I looked her up on Instagram. *@LexPotato . . . Oh my God, it's her.* Apparently she had seen my *Sh*t Valley Girls Say* video not too long ago, and when she visited Starbucks for Easter earlier that day, she thought of me. Just in case you didn't absorb that, SHE THOUGHT OF ME. I immediately asked her to go on a date with me that night, and she agreed. I drove to her house, picked her up, and kissed her almost immediately (I mean, technically we did wait three years).

Focus on things that make you happy.

So we've been together ever since. And every once in a while, I'll look her in the eyes, wrap my arms around her, and think about when we met for the first time three years ago, and I'll say, "You owe me seventy-five dollars."

A lot of people ask me how to get a boyfriend/girlfriend, and unfortunately there is no easy, one-size-fits-all answer. That's because most of the time it's about timing. If Lex had shown up to that first date at Coffee Bean, she probably wouldn't have liked me. I was young, immature, and just not ready for a girlfriend. I probably still would have liked *her*, but that's beside the point. And if we had reconnected any later, I may have been too caught up in work to even recognize how perfect she was for me. It's all about timing.

So if there is any concrete advice I can give you on how to get a girlfriend/boyfriend, the first piece is: Be patient. If you're not in a relationship at the moment, don't worry about it! Focus on things that make you happy, whether they be school, or friends, or even eating tacos at one a.m. (I don't know what you're into.) It usually takes time to find that perfect person, so make sure that the time *in between* is productive. It's that time that you invest in yourself that makes *you* appealing to so many people.

And the second bit of advice: If you don't try, you'll never succeed. Take chances and approach the person you're interested in; the worst thing they could do is set up a date at a Coffee Bean an hour away, then not show up, leaving you with a seventy-five-dollar parking ticket . . . but look how that turned out! My point is, that person you want to be in a relationship with (you know, the one you think is a demigod or a superhero) will never go out with you if you don't ask. Look at me: I would never have met Lex if I hadn't approached her (mom).

WHAT TO WEAR ON A FIRST DATE

by **Claudia Sulewski**

SHIRT:

Button-down shirts are great for first dates! If you're worried about feeling too overdressed, undo the top button and roll up your sleeves.

ACCESSORIES:

Don't be afraid of accessories! Throw on a simple watch and your favorite sunglasses to add a little flair.

PANTS:

Invest in some khaki pants. They are super soft and will melt any girl's heart if cuffed at the ankles. But seriously, these neutral pants are totally classic and walk that line of preppy and trendy.

SHOES:

When choosing shoes, stick to what you know best: casual sneakers! They'll help to balance out your outfit any time of the day.

FOR THE GUYS

JACKET:

Bring in dimension and color by throwing on a light jacket. Denim jackets give a classic vibe and go with almost anything!

PURSE:

Throw on your favorite bag for the cherry on top. You'll need to store your lip gloss and emergency mints somewhere. 😊

ACCESSORIES:

Less is more when it comes to jewelry. Stay away from overwhelming pieces that will distract your date! Simple bracelets and rings are always a great choice.

TOP:

A soft, loose-fitting T-shirt will never let you down. Wearing basic pieces lets you dress them down or up. I'm always grabbing for my trusty white V-neck

BOTTOMS:

I'm a firm believer in every girl owning a good ol' pair of black skinny jeans. Wear pieces that you know will be comfortable to walk around in. The less you focus on your look, the more you can focus on your date.

SHOES:

Shoes are the perfect way to add your own style and make a statement! Don't feel pressured to wear any crazy heels; squished toes and sore feet are not invited to this date. Throw on your favorite kicks or spice it up with some patterned slip-ons.

FOR THE LADIES

When I Knew . . .

Hunter March

(aka Lex's boyfriend)

Up until Lex, I had never really experienced *love*. Yeah, yeah, I had a girlfriend in high school who I said "I love you" to, and at the time I thought I meant it. But looking back, it wasn't love; it was just a combination of curiosity and infatuation that led to words being said and not understood.

Lex is the first person I've ever actually loved, and I knew almost immediately. That night we went out, exactly three years after meeting for the first time, I was beyond excited. I felt like a little boy on his first date ever. It felt like I had gotten the chance to not only meet my celebrity crush, but to go on a date and woo her. And woo I did.

We talked for hours. We talked about food, family, the Valley, college, my lack of college, anything and everything. And as you know, we kissed . . . and kissed some more. That's all you get to know.

When I dropped her off later that night, I was *not* in love. It was *way* too soon. You can't make a strong judgment in your life like that; you have to give it time. Let it grow. So I did.

The next morning, I was in love. I KNEW AND THAT WAS ALL THE TIME I NEEDED. When I woke up and realized I wanted to spend the entire day with her, I felt like Ryan Gosling in any movie he's ever been in. I couldn't focus on anything except Lex. Work? Nope. Sleep? Good luck. Hygiene? Yes, but only so Lex wouldn't smell the real me.

The problem was, I couldn't tell her yet. I thought it might freak her out if I called her the next morning and said, "Would you like to go on a second date? Great! Also, I'm in love with you. What movie do you want see?" So I shut my mouth.

We dated for months and that feeling never left, and that's when I started getting nervous. I felt like I'd stumbled upon this buried treasure and had it all to myself, but everyone else wanted it . . . because the treasure was super hot, smart, and funny. So three months into dating, a time long enough not to freak her out in my opinion, I decided to tell her.

In the middle of both of our workdays, I set up a lunch date at a restaurant in Santa Monica called Thyme Café because I couldn't wait until dinner. I picked her up in my car—the car that unfortunately smelled like crayons—and stared at her from the moment she got in, all while we ate, and up until leaving the restaurant. I was afraid she would disappear if I turned away, so I didn't.

The restaurant itself was too loud to say the fragile words, so we went out back to where we had parked and I stopped her. I grabbed her hands, and fumbled for five minutes because I was terrified, then I said, "I love you." Then we just stared at each other. A huge smile ran across her face. I thought, *This is it*. She opened her mouth and said, "You told me by a Dumpster?"

I turned and saw the Dumpster. It was right behind me. She did not say she loved me right then and there, but she would . . . hopefully.

When I Knew . . .

Lex Lee

(aka Hunter's girlfriend)

I think it's pretty cool that Hunter asked me to be in this book. He must really like me, right? I mean, this thing is published. You had to pay real money for it. It has, like, a binding and everything! AND he's letting ME say stuff in it!

Poop.

If that made the cut, he must REALLY love me.

That works out well, because I really love him. But I didn't know it until we took a trip to his parents' lake house in his 2004 Volkswagen Jetta that smelled like crayons. I went on this trip not knowing what we were or what we could be. We had only been "hanging out" for a few months and I was about to spend the weekend with his family.

It wasn't his six-pack, or the two other abs that make it an eight-pack, that made me fall in love with him . . . Sorry, Hunter grabbed the computer. But he's *right*, it wasn't that. Instead

OMG, I'm in love with a man in board shorts.

I fell in love with him when his mom made dinner that was so spicy it gave him a stomach-ache and rendered him completely useless. He was a blob on the couch all evening and it was so adorable to see your fearless author reduced to an eight-year-old boy in absolute agony.

This was when I fell. In. Love. But of course I couldn't tell him then. Especially not while he was doubled over in pain and wearing board shorts. I just kept thinking, *OMG, I'm in love with a man in board shorts*. But there is a difference from *knowing* you love them and actually *saying* it out loud with actual words.

You all know by now that he told me he loved me while we were next to a Dumpster, right? And how I didn't say it back? It wasn't because I didn't love him; I was just so shocked that he loved me. There is this window when someone tells you they love you in which you have to say it back without it sounding forced. And in my shock, I missed it, and so I held in my love for him as I held my nose . . . because, you know, the Dumpster thing.

I'll admit, having not said those three words back was like having a secret weapon. I knew his weakness (me) and he had yet to discover mine (dogs . . . I mean, him). But eventually the secret weapon turned on me. Finding the right moment became increasingly difficult, and as more time went by, the pressure was on to make it a memorable one. Several weeks had passed and I still played it cool. Yeah, Hunter, we get it, you love me. Meanwhile, inside my mind, I'm like, *I love you too, you big idiot.*

Then one night, we had a fight. In his car. Parked in his garage. After getting Thai food. What was the fight about? I have no idea. But I remember thinking *I can either continue to argue, or I can stop all this and just tell him how I really feel about him.* And just like that, I lifted my head up to face him and said, "You know I love you, right?" I officially lost the argument.

He started to crack a smile and said, "You decided to finally say it . . . during a fight?" I had no other recourse but to just kiss him. And I've been kissing him ever since. Even with tongue! He's gotten a lot better since his first kiss fiasco. Anyway, Hunter, if I'm ever upset with you, either because you deserve it or because I'm *hangry*, just show me this chapter. It might act as your *get out of jail free* card. Actually, it won't. But reminding me that I'm a published writer *will* make me feel better. I love you.

Poop, again.

—Lex

Final Forever

Aspyn Ovard

I never wanted a boyfriend in high school. I didn't see the point in dating someone seriously if I wasn't planning on marrying them, but I was not interested in that at the moment. In high school I wanted to keep my freedom, hang out with my friends, and just have fun. I knew I wasn't ready for a relationship. And then I met Parker.

It was the end of my sophomore year and we met through a mutual friend. He went to a different school but we happened to have a lot of friends in common. Immediately, however, I could sense that he wasn't like the other guys at my school. He was so sweet and nice . . . *again, not like the other guys at my school*. And that following summer, we became . . . close.

Hanging out with Parker was such a nice break from my chaotic schedule. Between going to school, making YouTube videos, and being a cheerleader, my high-stress mind loved his easygoing personality. Sure, we had tons in common too, but it was those important differences that just made it work.

We weren't exclusive . . . remember, I still wasn't ready to invest myself in a high-school relationship. But after months of casually hanging out, it hit me: *I don't want to kiss anyone else. I just kind of want to kiss Parker.* The next time we were hanging out, I wasn't sure how to tell him, so I just kind of blurted out, "Okay, you can be my boyfriend." Poetic? No. Eloquent? Not quite. Effective? Absolutely. He, being the sweet boy he was, turned it around on me by asking, "Aspyn, will you be my girlfriend?" And of course I said YES!!! This would be the first in a series of important "yes" responses in our relationship.

And then something completely unexpected happened . . .

The cool thing about falling in love with your friend is that it's not like they stop being your friend. It's like you have this boyfriend/best friend combo. They've seen all the good things and the bad things about you and they *still* decided that they want all of it. Sometimes your hair isn't going to be perfect, and yes, maybe sometimes you get angry for no reason. But since it's a part of what makes you who you are, they accept it. You don't have to pretend you're perfect, because you're perfect to them.

And Parker was perfect to me. It's hard to explain love. Like, if someone asked me why I love Parker, I could say the easy stuff, like he's the best, he's always the sweetest, and he's super cute. But that's not really even it. The best way I can describe it is I love him because he's Parker.

And while we were totally in love, I had completely forgotten one of the key reasons I didn't want a boyfriend in high school: What happens after graduation? I didn't have the traditional plan of going off to college. All I knew was that I would keep making YouTube videos and that I wanted to continue my relationship with Parker.

Parker, though, had other, more strict plans after graduation. He had always planned to go on a church mission after high school, but this wasn't like other missions. This mission would relocate him for TWO YEARS and communication was on a once-a-week basis. *Not your typical long-distance relationship.* I had full faith in our relationship, but TWO YEARS? That's rough for anyone.

It was a stressful summer to say the least. I decided to distract myself and plan a new life in Los Angeles. Moving day was fast approaching, but I just couldn't get excited. *And then something completely unexpected happened . . .* just one day too late. The day I signed my new lease in LA, Parker decided not to go on his mission. Ugh, life, right? I lasted four weeks in Los Angeles. FOUR weeks. I know, I know. I moved back home, but you know what? I don't have a single ounce of regret.

It was totally going to happen.

We spent the next year without the pressure of "what will happen next?" and were just free to be in *our* relationship. And it was the best.

That August we took a trip to Greece, and one night he told me he was going to cook dinner for me. He also mentioned that I should wear a cute dress. *It was totally going to happen.* I knew it. For better or worse, you just can't fool me. He led me through a candlelit path to our private dinner overlooking a beautiful view of the ocean. After our meal, he stood up and said . . . well, I don't exactly remember what he said because I was so nervous and my whole body was shaking. Then he got down on one knee, took out a ring, and asked me to marry him! Remember I said there was a series of important "yeses" in my future? Well, this was the BIG one.

I know right now you're thinking, *Okay, but you were, like, nineteen, why were you even thinking about forever?* Well, I'm not exactly your typical nineteen-year-old. YouTube has allowed me to have a wonderfully successful career, build and own a house, and travel the world!

And I was already making enough money to be financially independent from my parents. So even though I was young, I felt ready. I'm not saying it is for everybody, but it was our personal choice.

Marriage means being committed to that person forever, and I knew Parker was my forever. Yes, there are a lot, and I mean A LOT, of tough conversations to have and decisions to make before you get married. And we know that a lot of people probably thought we were like, "Oh, let's get married, it will be super fun." Let me be clear: It was NOT that easy.

I know a lot of you reading this aren't looking to get married so young, but the following piece of advice works for all stages of a relationship. Remember that you're going to change and evolve. Knowing who you are can be really hard when you're young. I feel like I've learned so much and grown so much even just from who I was a month ago! I'm constantly growing and changing, and so is Parker. That's something you have to think about: You want to make sure you are growing together. There are always going to be hard times, but if you love that person enough, then you will be able to work through everything together.

So, if you get married, or decide you *never* want to get married; if you want to have ten kids, one kid, no kids; if you want to go to Harvard, or not go to college at all; if you want to travel the world, or stay right where you are, do what feels right for *you*. There are so many different ways to live your life. But the most important thing is to ACTUALLY live your life.

For me, marrying Parker was just one of many things I wanted to do with mine.

What was the worst way you've broken up with someone, or worse . . . been broken up with? 😣

Claudia Sulewski
Breaking up over text. We've all been there as middle schoolers.

Alexis G. Zall
Same! Someone did it to me and it was like fifteen texts in a row of them explaining . . . whatever . . . and I responded "okay." And I think that was the best move ever if I do say so myself.

Andrew Lowe
Pass

LOL

Alex Aiono
I was dating a girl from back home, and she said she thought she wanted to break up, so I took a last-minute flight back to Arizona and took her flowers and candy to fix things . . . But she still dumped me . . . Hahaha.

Lauren Elizabeth
I called my boyfriend in the car when I was with the boy that I was going to be dating next. I broke up with him over speaker and he never knew the other guy was in the car with me . . . is that bad?

Yes. That's like the worst.

Maddy Whitby
In high school, I dated a boy for a year. Only problem was, I found out he was cheating on me but he refused to admit it. So I had to insist that he dump me because I knew he wanted to so bad. I basically broke up with myself for him.

Meg DeAngelis
This one guy in seventh grade had his friend do it. I didn't even know his friend. I was like "Who are you?" and he was like "I'm the guy telling you that your boyfriend is breaking up with you."

Ryan Abe
I found out my ex was cheating on me via Instagram.

Worst. Filter. Ever. 👎

What was your worst breakup?
Tweet me @HunterMarch with #TBHMyWorstBreakup

Getting Cheated On

I've always been a relationship kind of guy.

Think about it: You have someone who cares about you constantly. You have someone who actually *wants* to know how your day was. You have someone to share secrets with, someone to eat lunch with, and most important, someone to make out with. Relationships are the best . . . until they become the worst.

I began my first relationship when I was in my junior year of high school. And no, it was not with the girl who I shared my first kiss with. She never called me again. Was it because our kiss was too magical to ever re-create and the pressure scared her away from me? Probably not, but I do still tell myself that.

Anyway, growing up I always found it easy to talk to girls. Some people get terrified when they have to talk to someone of the opposite sex, but not me. It was actually a lot EASIER for me to talk to women than it was to talk to guys. With guys, I felt like I was competing. With women, I felt I was *completing* . . . them. ;) Joke too corny? Got it, okay.

I think the real reason I didn't talk to guys was because guys just aren't fans of talking. Women, on the other hand, seemed to love talking, and boy was I good at it.

As good as I was at talking to them, though, none of them seemed to want to date me. That was, until I met her. Her name was, well . . . because this story is kind of messed up, I'm going to change her name. We'll call her "Cheaty."

When I first saw Cheaty I was in shock. Cheaty was tall, Cheaty was beautiful, Cheaty had a lovely name that rhymed with Bamanda. So I approached her.

In all honesty, I really liked her. When we started talking, it felt natural and fun. She had a good sense of humor and we always made each other laugh. Eventually I made a move and we kissed, and it was everything I had ever hoped it would be, meaning, I used tongue this time—which is a real game changer, by the way. After that, I wanted to make her my girlfriend *officially.*

I held her hands, looked her in the eyes, and said, "Cheaty, would you be interested in making this official?"

She said, "Yes!"

We started going out on real dates, she met my family, I met hers, and I ditched school (the one and only time) to hang out with her while she was out sick. It was . . . magic.

But then I remembered that magic isn't real. And in case you forgot, this chapter is called *GETTING CHEATED ON!* So about a year in, I started noticing stuff that made me suspicious. She would get texts and hide them from me, or delete them altogether, which, unless she was throwing me a surprise birthday party, was NOT a good sign.

Then I started getting paranoid, and I started sneaking looks at her phone, then she'd catch me and make *me* feel like I was doing something wrong. *Why couldn't I trust my own girl-friend? Why would I ever suspect such horrible things?* Oh yeah, BECAUSE HER NAME WAS CHEATY!

After about a year of me being suspicious and her doing suspicious things, two of my classmates pulled me aside during lunch one day and told me that they'd definitely seen her cheating on me at a party the previous night . . . with someone I knew well. It felt like I was hit by a truck. The air left my body, I felt sick, then I asked for details, and painfully got them. But I still needed *her* to admit to it; I don't know why that was so important, but it was. So I came up with a plan.

It felt like
I was
hit by a
truck.

That day I went to her house and told her that I had stopped by a party the day before, and *saw* everything. With every intimate detail I gave her, *that my classmates had actually given me,* her mouth dropped lower and lower. I didn't ask her if it was true, because that would've given her an out; instead I asked her *why*. And she told me. Then I didn't ask her if this was the only time; instead I asked her how long this had been going on. And she told me. Then I thought about the other times I was suspicious and brought those up. She was like *Usher's Confessions Parts 1* and *2* at this point, revealing to me the truth about every-thing she ever said I was "acting crazy" about.

At the end of our talk, I had found out that she had cheated on me multiple times, with multiple people, all of whom I had suspected and asked her about at one point in the rela-tionship. It was heartbreaking. Like I literally thought my heart had broken. I also felt like an idiot because a bunch of other people knew before I did. I didn't have anyone to turn to because I was embarrassed that I had been cheated on in the first place. I felt like me being a bad boyfriend, for whatever reason, contributed to all of this happening to me.

I should've seen the signs from a million miles away, but I didn't; my mind was preoccupied by our mouth wrestling.

First sign: My mom didn't like her. Neither did my brother, or anyone in my life for that mat-ter. I chalked it up to parents not understanding, but honestly, my mom knows everything past, present, and future about my life. Had I just listened to her when she said that this girl wasn't right for me, I could have avoided an entire year of getting cheated on!

Second sign: Her need to hide *everything* from me. Whether it was text messages or *friends* that she was visiting, I was never allowed to be part of it. I thought at the time that it was just a part of her personal life, and that I should give her that space, but it ended up being much more than that. I learned that when you're with someone in a *healthy* relationship, there shouldn't need to be any secrets.

And finally, the ultimate sign that I was getting cheated on was always having the feeling I was getting cheated on. To make it worse, that paranoia destroys trust, which is (excuse the cliché) the foundation of any relationship. Without that trust, I never fully committed to that person, and in the long run, I was never truly happy.

Being cheated on is one of the most heartbreaking things a person can go through. You give your all to someone, and they take it, crumple it up, and throw it in the trash. That one act can leave a leave a ton of wounds.

If that's ever happened to you, I'm sorry. I know how horrible this all feels and it left me with serious trust issues. I kept people at a distance, avoided any serious connection, and was just generally okay with being single. Then I met someone who changed everything, and that person is still my girlfriend today. For this story I will call her Trusty.

INSTRUCTION MANUAL FOR GETTING OVER A BREAKUP

Congratulations! You have purchased a gut-wrenching breakup kit. When applied effectively, our kit increases the chances that you will be okay. Because you will be.

EACH KIT INCLUDES:

31,784,413 pieces of a broken heart (pieces vary by user)

1 pair of cozy sweatpants

1 overwhelming sensation that there will never be a reason to wear anything other than sweatpants. Ever.

A comfortable place to lie down

A breakup playlist that just gets you

(At least) 1 really good friend

Tears (amount varies by user)

An endless supply of word vomit

Some space

1 bad decision. Options vary but may include the following:

- An extreme haircut
- A piercing your parents will not approve of
- An entire Costco-size bag of Doritos
- A make-out session with that sketchy kid in your math class
- A spree of text messages to your ex

Time (again, amount varies by user)

STEP 1: PICK UP THE PIECES

Wrap the pieces of your broken heart in bubble wrap and place them in a drawer. You're not ready to assemble them yet.

STEP 2: WALLOW

Apply your cozy sweatpants and hunker down on the couch. Liberally dole out tears as if they're going out of style.

STEP 3: PHONE A FRIEND

Once you've hit the emotional state where you simultaneously want to claw your way back into your ex's heart and claw their eyes out, you need backup. Call your friend and word vomit all of these feelings an unreasonable amount.

STEP 4: UNFRIEND YOUR EX

You may be able to be friends with your ex eventually . . . but not yet. This is where you must employ "some space" and stop texting/hanging out with your ex. (If you really want to max-imize this phase, it wouldn't hurt to stop following their social media—you can re-follow to stalk them later.)

STEP 5: MAKE A BAD DECISION

Once you've cut off your ex, it's time to make your bad decision. The breakup is still fresh enough that everyone will pretend to like your haircut/piercing/Dorito-stained fingers. Wait too long, and all these things stop being cute.

STEP 6: ADJUST TO BEING A "ME"

Being a "we" comes with its perks, but being a "me" can be awesome, even if it doesn't feel like it right now. The more you distract yourself from feeling alone, the better you will get at actually being alone. For a list of suggestions, see DISTRACTIONS FROM A BREAKUP, page 164.

STEP 7: STOP THE WORD VOMIT

At a certain point, talking about how good it feels to be "over it" actually prevents you from getting over it. Find a willing friend and spend fifteen minutes saying everything it is you really feel like you need to say about your ex. When the fifteen minutes are done, so are you.

STEP 8: TAKE YOUR TIME

Ultimately the only thing that really helps you get over heartbreak is time. Then one day, you'll accidently open a drawer looking for a pencil and you'll find that the pieces of your heart have managed to put themselves back together. Without even really noticing, you'll just be okay.

My Almost Relationship

I've been in only one relationship that I consider serious, and—luckily—I'm still in it. Sure, I've had other relationships, some short ones that ended with mutual ghosting, and one in high school where my girlfriend confused a bunch of other guys for me. That one was particularly devastating, breakups always are, but the breakup that actually hurt the most wasn't even with a girlfriend, it was with an *almost* girlfriend.

We've all been there. You start talking to someone and it's perfect and magical, but then it ends before any actual commitment is made. That's an *almost* girlfriend or boyfriend. My almost girlfriend happened right out of high school with a girl I met on Instagram named "Samantha."

She played volleyball, she was beautiful, and most important to me at the time, she and I had mutual friends on Facebook. One of those mutual friends was my brother, who I immediately started pelting with questions. Those questions yielded two key pieces of information: First, they went to school together. Second, he was 80 percent sure she was single, which were odds I was willing to gamble with. So I followed her on Instagram, commented on a picture, she commented back, we DM'd each other, and I wasted absolutely zero time setting up a date.

From the moment I picked her up at her house, we started cracking each other up. There is nothing more attractive to me than someone with a sense of humor, and boy did she have one. Not only did she pick up on every joke I sent her way, but she sent them right back! Oh, and she was smart. Like scholarship smart. Meanwhile, I'm, like, *almost* community college smart, so this was a perfect match.

I took her to this romantic Italian restaurant in the area, and after hours of laughing like we were the only people in the place, I joked that she should take the last, giant meatball on our plate, put it onto a serving spoon, hold it up to the waiter, and ask if she could take it to go, no doggie bag necessary, she had a spoon. It was beyond stupid, and should've revealed me

It. Was. ~~Magical.~~ Awkward.

as the weirdo I was, but she actually did it! And while the bewildered waiter walked toward his manager to ask about our ridiculous request, we were crying tears of laughter.

That continued for the rest of the night, until I walked her to her door and accidentally met her parents. This would usually be an awkward end to a first date, but they were actually a lot of fun! They liked me and I liked them and I liked her and *ahhh*. You know that feeling.

After that crown jewel of a first date, I figured that it was only a matter of time before she realized that we were in love and we became an official couple. So we set up another date, and again it was hilarious and involved Italian food, and at the end of it, I went in for the kiss we had both been waiting for.

It. Was. ~~Magical~~. Awkward. But honestly, what first kiss isn't?? Not everything is a Ryan Gosling movie, and I figured we would just try again on another date. So I texted her and asked her if she wanted to get another spoonful of spaghetti to go, but she was busy. And then she stayed pretty busy for a while. Sometimes it was school, sometimes her team . . . I guess I just didn't realize how many away games there were in a volleyball season.

After weeks of trying, we set up another date, and after yet another fun night of nonstop laughter, I went in for the second kiss. I figured our first kiss was like three seconds, so this one would be at least like six seconds. Math, right? Wrong. It was zero seconds. I got rejected. Not like a blatant LeBron James in your face rejection, more like a turn of the head and change of the subject rejection.

That's when it all started falling apart. I felt us drifting a little and I desperately wanted to hold on. It was like we were on ships moving in different directions. Or she was on a ship and I was on one of those little dinghies. Or maybe it was like the *Titanic* had sunk and I was Jack holding on to that piece of plywood, but instead of her being like, "I'll never let go, Jack," she was just like, "Bye."

A few weeks later, our lol-inducing text messages were getting farther and farther apart, and then she posted a selfie on Instagram where she was posed with another guy's arm around her. The photo caption was something about a pool party, but all I read was "Sorry, Hunter, but I'm going to get Italian food to go with *this* guy from now on."

The worst part was that the guy didn't look funny at all. He looked like one of those handsome guys who never had to be funny in his life because women always liked him for his biceps. I knew I could make her laugh way more than this guy; just look how small my biceps are!

I racked my brain for reasons this might've happened; what did I do wrong? Was I a bad kisser? *I can't have been that bad. You can't tell in three seconds, can you?* Maybe I just wanted it too much and in my desperation to make it happen, I made it *not* happen.

I wanted to talk to my friends about it, but this was a situation I couldn't bring up to anyone I knew. When you've been dumped, your friends rally around you. They come over, bring junk food, and talk about how dumb your ex is for letting you go. They make mean jokes about him or her that don't really make you feel better but at least make you feel like someone has your back. But the same is *not* true when your ex doesn't even know that they're your ex. Then it goes something like this:

> Hunter: *We broke up. It's done.*
> Friend: *Don't worry, man, I brought ice cream. Are you okay?*
> Hunter: *Nope, and honestly, I don't know if I ever will be.*
> Friend: *I'm so sorry. How long were you guys together?*
> Hunter: *Technically? If you add it all up, about zero days.*
> Friend: . . .
> Hunter: . . .
> Friend: *Give me back my ice cream.*

When people think of heartbreak, most of the time they focus on losing the person they had and all the memories that came with them. But heartbreak isn't entirely about losing what *was*. It's also about losing what *could've been*.

Sure, you'll miss the time you shared licorice together at the movies, your first kiss in your backyard, but you'll also miss what hadn't happened yet: the prom you never went to together, the camping trip you never went on, or the second kiss you never had.

Whether the relationship lasted ten years, ten minutes, or, in my case, not at all, what you're really trying to get over is the future you *almost* had, but didn't. It's the loss of an idea. I realize now that I wasn't really upset about losing her; I was upset that I lost the relationship *I thought was possible* with her, and that loss was very real to me.

Most heartbreak comes before relationships even start. That's why crushes are called crushes, because when it's all over you feel *crushed*. So if you've ever been there, you are not alone. I'm right there with you, and if you ever want to talk about it, I know a great Italian restaurant.

DISTRAC-TIONS FROM A BREAKUP

1

NETFLIX BINGE.

You know that movie you missed because your ex didn't like plots about clowns with machetes? Spoiler alert! Now is your time to catch up. (Also, everyone dies.)

2

REORGANIZE YOUR CLOSET.

After a breakup is a great time to get rid of other stuff in your life that was holding you back. And if you find any of your ex's stuff and have the urge to set it on fire, just make sure you don't do it indoors or in a densely wooded area. Only you can prevent breakup-related forest fires.

3

NETFLIX REWIND.

Remember that show that was your *favorite* show when you were in the fifth grade? This is a great time to rewatch it. It'll remind you of a simpler time before your ex did jumping jacks on your heart.

4

MAKE PLANS.

The temptation to throw yourself an epic pity party is strong. Fight it by filling up your calendar! Go to the movies with friends. Go to an *actual*, nonpity party. Even help your mom with that thing in the garage she's been asking you to do for like a year. So while your ex is spending all his or her time realizing what a mistake he or she made, you'll be too busy planning your next adventure to care.

5

SET A PERSONAL GOAL.

Whether your goal is to run a marathon, learn to cook, or even just to make it to the next level in *Halo 27*, not only will it give you something to focus on other than your breakup, achieving that goal will build confidence. And nothing is hotter than confidence.

6

DID I MENTION NETFLIX?

How do you distract yourself from a breakup?
Tweet me @HunterMarch with #TBHBestBreakupDistractions

Love Yourself

Lauren Elizabeth Luthringshausen

When I was in high school—no, make that middle school—I became obsessed with the idea of love. I always thought of love as a perfect relationship with a perfect boy—like in the movies. I fell in love with the idea of love. So I guess you could say I've been a hopeless romantic since I was very young. I remember sitting on the swings with my childhood best friend listing off each boy I liked in each grade! And then finally, in my senior year ethics class, I learned what love really takes. My teacher explained the difference between love and infatuation, and that difference was WORK. Literally, that was the answer to a question on a test, I'm 100 percent positive—okay, 99 percent, but still!! LOVE = WORK. That's what I wrote down in my notebook.

For me, that was great news. Not only was I a hopeless romantic, I was a hard worker. Even in high school, I was always working on blog posts, videos, networking, and taking over the city of Chicago at eighteen. Everything I've accomplished in my career is because of my strong work ethic. I don't take no for an answer and always figure out a way to succeed. So as I grew up, I never really let any of the boys I thought I loved (or loved the idea of) go, because I thought if I could just work hard enough I could make any relationship into that perfect relationship I fantasized about. Let me shatter that illusion for you right now—that perfect relationship doesn't exist. But I didn't know that yet.

Flashback to my first real love. I had just turned twenty years old when I met the guy who would be my boyfriend for nearly two years. A mutual friend had been trying to set us up for a while because she thought we would hit off, and she was right; when I saw him, I knew immediately. I felt it.

For our first date we went to a sushi place and stayed for almost four hours just talking nonstop. We went back to my apartment at the time and I took him up on the roof. It was a beautiful night and we sat on the roof till two a.m. just talking about life. I knew then that I loved him and could see a future with him. We didn't even kiss for the first couple of weeks (he was such a gentleman). He would pick me up and take me on simple, cute dates. One time he surprised me and took me to a bookstore because he remembered I mentioned I loved reading and couldn't find a store around me. One night we went to a concert together and had our first kiss. It was magical, and we woke up the next morning like we would every weekend to come for the next year. I wanted to be with him all the time.

In the past it was so easy for me to pick people apart and see their flaws. But when I fell in love, you guessed it, I couldn't see anything but perfection. In reality he had quit his job, so he was financially unstable; he was totally emotionally unavailable; he lived with his parents about twenty miles away (which, with LA traffic, is basically a long-distance relationship); and even when we could be together, he sometimes chose to hang out with his friends or go to the gym instead of be with me. Still, he was perfect to me: Everything I'd ever wanted and more I didn't even know I wanted. I supported him quitting his job to pursue his dream. I told myself I didn't mind that we couldn't see each other a lot during the week because we would talk every night. And even on the weekends, I'd let him do his thing and would sit and wait for him to return, because I didn't mind; I was going to make this work.

While I knew the moment we locked eyes with each other that we'd fall in love, I don't think he ever planned on that happening. But he couldn't help it, it just happened. So when we said I love you for the first time, I remember having to pry it out of him because he was scared. I wasn't. I insisted that it was okay and that we could make it all work. But even when he said I love you without provocation, he wasn't ready to attach himself to someone else. Meanwhile, I attached myself right away and loved him with everything I had. That's when the work began to overshadow the love. It's hard planning your life around someone else, especially as you're trying to grow into yourself as a person as well as a couple. We were truly in love. Of that I was and am certain. But because I wanted that perfect relationship so badly, I wasn't letting things happen organically and we began to resent each other. Then seven months in, he broke up with me.

I figured it didn't work because I wasn't working hard enough. So I decided I was going to work harder. I sent him texts upon texts about how he had made a mistake and met up with him multiple times. He would ask me how things could be different. And I would offer suggestion after suggestion: I could drive to him, he could stay with me more, we didn't even need to see each other some days! It could work! I was willing to do anything!! We got back together and we were making a lot of progress, but I kept forcing him to put a label on it. "Do you love me? Do you want this?" Every single weekend I would literally cry when he left because I felt like nothing without him, I wanted to be with *him* every single day. But suddenly I realized I didn't want to be around *me*.

I love him. But do I love myself? That was probably a question that never crossed my mind back then. I channeled everything I had into making our relationship work and in doing so totally ignored my own needs. So I began taking care of myself. I started therapy again for the first time since high school for my overwhelming anxiety. I felt crazy, like I wasn't even a real person anymore. I began to feel hopeless. And after months of resisting, I agreed to go on medication. And as someone who has dealt with depression before, I didn't want to go even farther down the road I was heading. So I took care of myself. Saw the doctors. Took the medicine. Started doing things I had always wanted to do with him, on my own. I finally felt like I could do things without him. For example, I had always wanted to get a puppy with him because I was afraid I couldn't handle it by myself. But I did get a puppy and it was the best decision I ever made. I started hanging out with MY friends again, not just his. I started putting more energy into myself and I started growing stronger and stronger. I got to a point where I wasn't crying when he was leaving and I was confused: *Do I not care about him?*

Slowly I realized I had spent so much time thinking about what I could work on I didn't really think about the things that he was working on. Which is in retrospect was . . . nothing. He wasn't really working at all. I had worked to accept his flaws but he hadn't really accepted mine. For me, my flaw is being insecure. I'm insecure when it comes to being loved and believing the affirmations I'm given. All I wanted was for him to say the RIGHT thing. When I was sad, I just wanted him to look me in the eyes and say, *Lauren, I love you, I am always going to be here for you; we are in this together.* He didn't do that. He didn't really even try. And that's when I realized there was one thing I was doing wrong. I was making excuses for him. I would convince myself I didn't need more quality time or I didn't need someone to profess his love to me every day. In my mind his resistance to saying, *I love you, Lauren. We're a TEAM*, was just him being a guy! I was genuinely in denial.

Finally I got to a point where I was like, What am I doing? I need someone who can love me the way I need to be loved. And for the first time I thought maybe that wasn't him. I came to this insane epiphany one night over a cheese platter with my two best friends. I said, "I think I just spent so much time loving him and putting everything I had into him, because I didn't love myself." We all looked at one another just like, WHOA . . . I had finally said it out loud and it became real. I finally loved myself, like, REALLY loved myself. And I knew what I deserved, so I laid down the law with him and said he and I needed some space to think about if we really wanted this. And he didn't fight for me. And that was it.

Growing up and until that moment, love was worth everything to me. Without love, life was a failure. Without love, what had I accomplished? I needed love to be validated, to have a purpose. I had ingrained this idea in myself that I needed to grow up, get a job, and find love because without love, how do you spend your whole life after high school?! Oh, Lauren . . . young, young Lauren. *eye roll*

Now I'm not saying love isn't important, I'm just asking, What is love WORTH? *Is it worth all that work? Is not being fully loved worth settling for? Because your life is defined by love, right? So is it worth it? No.* I believe if you truly love someone, you feel 100 percent confident answering the question, What does love mean? If you aren't being loved fully, you probably aren't sure of your answer . . . I truly believe the older you get, the more you learn about love: what it really means, what it really takes, and what it's really worth.

But I think the biggest piece of it is that in order to figure out how you need to be loved, you need to love yourself. I got a part of it right when I was younger. Life is about love. But it's about self-love. That's the real work that needs to be done. It's about being able to know that you're enough. Even if you get insecure, even if you sometimes pronounce words wrong, or get weird lint between your toes, you are an awesome, unique, and beautiful person and you deserve someone who sees all of that and thinks, *Wow, that's the person for me.* When I did that, I learned I need a partner who is going to accept my insecurities and learn how to affirm me in a way that makes me feel safe. Sounds easy, right? Yeah, well, apparently not. But hey, I'm just an angsty single girl looking for love, so I might be biased. ;)

ULTIMATE BREAKUP PLAYLIST

If Beyoncé has taught us anything, it's that when life gives you lemons, you make a platinum album. Just look at the reigning breakup philosopher of our time, Taylor Swift. She uses songs to work out feelings about old relationships so she can move on to newer (and cuter) ones. And even if you're not T. Swift talented, you can still use music to get over a breakup. Sometimes a bad breakup just needs a good breakup mix.

1. "STITCHES" BY SHAWN MENDES

Every breakup is different. If you had one of those breakups that hurts so badly you feel like your heart has been torn into a million pieces and then those pieces were put in a wood chipper, this is your first track. Shawn Mendes understands how it feels when your heart needs to be stitched back together, and he's surprisingly upbeat about it.

2. "I KNEW YOU WERE TROUBLE" BY TAYLOR SWIFT

If you think you should have seen your breakup coming, this song kicks off your breakup mix. Sometimes you fall in love so hard that you can't see the signs of trouble. But now that you've hit the ground *hard*, don't blame yourself. This song is a comforting reminder that everyone makes mistakes—even Taylor Swift.

3. "BEFORE HE CHEATS" BY CARRIE UNDERWOOD

If your relationship ended because your ex was a horrible cheater named Cheaty McCheaterson, you *need* this country hit. What better way to start your breakup mix than the ultimate revenge-against-your-ex song. It's all of the fun of destroying your ex's stuff, without any of the jail time!

4. "WRECKING BALL" BY MILEY CYRUS

So things are over but you're not, like, *ready* for them to be over. When you think about your ex, this flood of emotions hits you like a bus or a ton of bricks, or, well . . . "Wrecking Ball" is perfect for when you're ready to scream and cry and maybe throw things but you're still not quite ready to let go.

5. "SHAKE IT OUT" BY FLORENCE + THE MACHINE

That whole "don't cry because it's over, smile because it happened," thing might be clichéd, but it's also kind of true. Right now memories of your relationship may be constantly haunting you, but regrets are worthless. You *will* get over this and, as Florence says, it's always darkest before the dawn.

6. "LOVE YOURSELF" BY JUSTIN BIEBER

For that moment when you realize that you really are better off without your ex, but still kind of want to tell them to go . . . love themselves.

7. "CLEAN" BY TAYLOR SWIFT

You know when it's a been a few months since your breakup and you realize, *Huh, I haven't thought about my ex in a while* and their name briefly floating through your head does **not** cause the immediate desire to eat a large quantity of cookie dough? That's what "Clean" is about: the moment when you realize you are ACTUALLY over it. You've learned what you needed from the experience, you've cried your tears, and you've achieved all your #squadgoals.

8. "SURVIVOR" BY DESTINY'S CHILD

You did it! You survived your breakup. Beyoncé and I are very proud of you. And there is literally no song better or more empowering to blast at full volume when you want to celebrate your independence than this classic throwback.

What's on your breakup mix?
Tweet me **@HunterMarch** with **#TBHBestBreakupSong**

FRIENDSHIP
FAMILY LOVE
SCHOOL
HEARTBREAK
Hustles
INSECURITIES
STRUGGLES

Okay, TBH, we have the best jobs ever. But I want to know . . . what was your WORST job?

Lauren Elizabeth Driving around in a car with Hunter. #ThirdWheel

Again, that falls under "best job ever."

Alex Aiono I worked only one job outside of music and YouTube, and it was selling women's clothing. So between those, that was definitely my worst job, haha.

Maddy Whitby Monica and I applied to one of those "trying to be hip" retail stores in the mall and in the joint interview they were like, "Yeah, chill, you can work here now or whatever." I cleaned the front windows for three hours and never went back.

Monica Sherer I remember that. I just folded the same stacks of T-shirts over and over again. Neither one of us even quit, we just stopped going in.

I wonder if they still think you work there . . .

Ryan Abe I worked at a Lone Star Steakhouse and I had to pick up the peanut shells that people would throw on the floor. I still don't understand. There's a bucket right there! USE THE BUCKET!

Katherine Cimorelli I had to clean my dad's boxing gym, aka all the sweat, blood, and dirt everywhere, for NOTHING. Yeah, it wasn't exactly a job, lol. I scrubbed so many toilets.

Aija Mayrock I once babysat five kids and three dogs, then I accidentally fell asleep and when I woke up, the kids were drawing on the walls with permanent marker . . .

Veronica Merrell Babysitting for me too. Vanessa and I would babysit at our church. The babies just cry and then it would start a chain reaction of crying and then I'd want to cry. 😣

Have a worst-job story?
Tweet me @HunterMarch with #TBHMyWorstJob

First Job

Unless your parents are royalty (either like British royalty or the Kardashians) there comes a time in your life when you need to get a job. I personally knew I had reached that point when my mom sat me down, looked me in the eyes, and said, "You need to get a job." For some reason, when I graduated from high school, she was suddenly *not so cool* with giving me free money to do whatever I wanted. I didn't get it either, like, she was my mom. That's when I realized it was time for me to become an adult.

I went out into the world and started looking for that next chapter of life experience! I put on my only shirt that didn't have a logo on the front, filled out countless résumés, and got zero responses. The only place to contact me back called to say that they were looking for someone with more experience. *WHAT?!* For one, a text would've been fine. And two, that's crazy! The reason I didn't *have experience* was because I couldn't get a job. And the reason I couldn't get a job was because I didn't have experience! As an adult now, I realize that's life, but at the time I was so upset. I vented to my dad about the unsuccessful job hunt while on our weekend Starbucks stop.

You know those people who are at Starbucks *every* day? Like, being at Starbucks at a certain time is basically in their calendar? Well, that guy you're thinking of right now might be my dad. Ever since I was a kid, Starbucks was a regular thing for us. He would say, "It's the one thing that makes me happy every day that I can actually afford." He's never had a lot of money, but a basic cup of Starbucks coffee costs about two bucks, which was in his price range.

On one of these ritual Starbucks trips, I told my dad that I couldn't get a job to save my life, and before I could even finish my rant about unobtainable experience, he stood up and left me. *Not really the best time, Dad!* Then he came back and said, "You have an interview at this Starbucks tomorrow afternoon."

And right then, I became an adult.

Whoa. To me, Starbucks was an unreachable mecca of decent pay, health benefits, and free cinnamon rolls. And I had an interview there the next day. So I went home and did what every kid does: I Googled *what to do during a job interview.*

Then I went to the interview, and KILLED it. The manager I spoke with loved me, she told my dad that they would be hiring me immediately, and right then, I became an adult. An adult who loved Caramel Frappuccinos (easy on the coffee, heavy on the caramel). No matter what it is, a first job teaches you a lot of things that you can apply to almost any trade thereafter. Here are some lessons I learned:

DON'T DATE CUSTOMERS

I thought Starbucks was going to be a mecca for meeting women. I mean, if they wanted their latte, they literally *had* to talk to me. Problem was, most women ordering Starbucks don't want to date the guy making it. I guess you don't sip where you eat. That became truly apparent to me when one specific girl came in and we started talking. We were both eighteen, were both living in the area, and were both worried about me spelling her name correctly on the cup. Before she left, I gave her my phone number on a cup sleeve because I didn't have my phone on me to ask for hers. Perfect.

Ten minutes later her father walked in, asked to speak with me, and handed me back the cup sleeve with my phone number on it, completely ripped to shreds. He said he was a traditional man and that I should ask *him* if I could ask his daughter out first. So while trying not to pee myself out of fear, I asked *him* if I could ask his daughter out. He said no, then walked out. He rejected me so hard.

DON'T DATE COWORKERS

After a *talking-to* from my manager, I stopped flirting with customers for a bit and instead started seeing a coworker. That ended up being an even *worse* idea. Under normal circumstances, when you stop dating someone that you only went on a couple of dates with, you never have to see them again. There's an unspoken agreement that either you'll become friends and pretend the dates never happened or you'll just pretend the other person doesn't exist at all. But you can't do that with coworkers. Because you have to, you know, *cowork* with them. When my fellow barista and I stopped seeing each other, her normal conversations with me got mean, even in front of customers. I don't want to say which one of us had to leave the store because of complaints, but it wasn't me . . . because it was her. She had to leave the store because she was yelling at me in front of customers. But, again, I won't say which of us had to leave.

THE CUSTOMER IS ALWAYS RIGHT (EVEN WHEN THEY'RE WRONG)

The most basic rule of the service industry, especially Starbucks, is that the customer is ALWAYS right. And at Starbucks it's the worst because people get extremely, almost unnecessarily specific. *You want a 193-degree, three-and-a-half pump, half-caf Caramel Macchiato with no foam, nonfat whipped cream, and for me to spell your fifteen-character name right? No problem!* It was part of my job to make sure the customer was right, except for that one time when I told a customer that he was wrong . . .

True story, a guy and his family walked in asking for four Venti Frappuccinos with exactly fifteen ice cubes in each. Because there is no difference between fifteen ice cubes and sixteen ice cubes, and since it's unsanitary to touch ice cubes with your hands, I just eyeballed the amount. Ten minutes later the guy came back and said that I had made them with too many ice cubes, and insisted I make them again; also, he was going to keep the old Frappuccinos. I told him I couldn't because he'd already drunk the first ones. The guy lost his mind, called my manager, and eventually I had to remake the Frappuccinos with *exactly* fifteen ice cubes in each. I gained nothing by telling him he was wrong and almost got fired in return. Was it the right decision to tell him he was wrong? No. But if we're being honest, which we are, fifteen ice cubes is ridiculous and I hope that guy is reading this.

But the biggest mistake I learned from that job was actually from working *too* hard. Toward the end of my first year there, I was asking for every extra shift I could, doing overtime even when I wasn't asked, and trying to be the employee of the month, every day. I wanted the money, but it was draining every other part of my life. My grades fell, I stopped talking to some of my friends, and I did *not* like who I was becoming. That's when I realized, *I don't want to work here my whole life.* I didn't know what I wanted to do, but I knew it wasn't this. So I took a chance and quit making people coffee to pursue something that made me happy. I wasn't sure exactly what that was going to be yet, but I knew it wasn't a fifteen-ice-cube Frappuccino.

The $64,000 Question

When I started at AwesomenessTV, I was not the experienced host you've (hopefully) seen on the *Daily Report, #DearHunter, Third Wheel, Top Five Live,* or any number of the other shows I've hosted. I mean, I completely wanted to be that experienced host; I was just missing the experience part. Instead, on camera, I was awkward, talked way too fast, and had a horrible haircut. But I was determined to be the best host there ever was; I mean, it was in my blood.

In the 1950s my grandfather hosted a TV show called *The $64,000 Question* and a radio show called *Sweeny and March.* You guessed it: He was the March portion and his name was Hal. For hosting both of those shows, he was given *two* stars on the Hollywood Walk of Fame and a career that most entertainers only dream of. My grandfather always knew what he wanted, went after it, and got it.

But for most of my young life I had no idea what I wanted! Picking a career became the $64,000 question of my life. Whenever I was asked about it in class, I would give the basic answers, like fireman. But if I'm being honest, there was no way I was going into a building that was on fire; I get scared when my marshmallow catches fire while camping. I also told teachers that I wanted to be a professional athlete. Problem there was that I weighed like twenty pounds less than every other kid my age and wasn't interested in the *practice* portion of sports, which apparently is important if you want to be a pro.

The only thing I did like at that time was being the center of attention. I'm not kidding when I tell you there's a video of me yelling the ABCs as loud as I can in my front yard. *Why?* It wasn't because I was asked to, it wasn't because I thought the ABCs was the most banging song of the year; it was simply because my dad was filming me.

Somewhere in those moments, the ones where I got to try to make my family laugh, I realized I wanted to be a performer. I don't know how, or when it clicked, *but it clicked hard.* Every situation became a chance to show people how funny I was. Teachers hated it, but my classmates . . . well, they seemed to hate it too. Unfortunately for my dreams of performing, I couldn't sing, dance, or play an instrument, and therefore had nothing *worth* performing.

When the high school talent show came around sophomore year, I was kind of devastated. All I wanted to do was be on that stage, making people laugh, but instead just hid in the back and quietly watched other people audition. I LOVE watching performers onstage, even if they are high school kids all singing the same John Mayer song. Then, in between two different versions of "Gravity," they brought up a kid to audition to be the *host of the show.* My mind started racing. *That's a position they audition for? I feel like you don't need to have any talent for that role . . . I mean, I have no talent, I could do that! I could beat that talentless kid!*

So I asked to audition, ran onto the stage when my name was called, and realized that being a host actually requires a ton of talent. I bombed. In all the excitement of being up there with ten other kids watching me, I messed up the words, asked to start over twice, and dropped the mic . . . by accident, like not in the cool way at all. The only thing worse than what I did onstage was apparently what that other kid did onstage because I GOT THE PART!

They specifically told me that my only job was to read the names of the upcoming performers in between acts. But what I *heard* was, *Hunter, this is your show. The acts are just there to give **you** time to prepare your next hilarious segment. The entire talent show is riding on your shoulders, sir.*

So I went to work. For weeks I planned and planned what I would do to fill up this hour of entertainment. I recruited people into my act, learned how to juggle, and bought a magic set. I was ready to make some *talent* magically appear.

All I wanted to do was be on that stage.

I knew that this was what I was meant to do.

When the big day came, though, I was terrified. The entire student body and their parents were in the auditorium, and it was time for me to open the show. My ears were ringing, the microphone slipping in my wet palms, and my haircut was still awful; then my introductory Katy Perry song stopped. It was my time to go. *Time to get on out there. Just move your feet, Hunter . . .* I was stuck. I stood at the wing of the stage, paralyzed; then my principal gave me a really aggressive look and I snapped out of it, running onto the stage. Immediately, the lights replaced all my jitters and nerves with pure adrenaline. It was time to perform.

Every laugh, smile, and *ahhh* I got was like a shot of happiness. All the hard work I'd done was paying off with actual reactions from a real audience. After doing a bit where I pretended I was about to juggle a baby, a football, and a chain saw, I knew that *this* was what I was meant to do . . . no, not the baby juggling. I was meant to be a *host*!

Some people pick their career sooner than that, others go through most of their life before they figure it out, but I guarantee you it will happen. If you're having trouble deciding what to do with your life, don't worry! Just focus on what makes you happy. Forget about whether it will make you money, forget about whether your parents want you doing it, just make sure it's something you could do with a genuine smile on your face. Also, make sure it's legal.

For me, that passion is undoubtedly performing in front of as many people as I can. Although my grandfather Hal died before I ever had the chance to meet him, my dad told me story after story about his legendary father. I feel like I know him, like he was guiding me through all of this, and all I hope is that he's proud of what I'm doing . . . even if he has no idea what YouTube is.

Becoming Awesome...ness

It's one thing to realize what you want to do for the rest of your life. It's another thing *altogether* to actually do it.

Now, sure, there are those rare stories where someone just gets plucked out of obscurity and thrown into the best job ever for the rest of their lives. For example, Harrison Ford was a carpenter when he got the part of Han Solo in a little movie called *Star Wars*. And Mark Zuckerberg just so happened to start a little website in his college dorm room that launched him from ramen-eating college student to tech billionaire. But if we're being honest, you didn't invent Facebook, and you're not going to be Han Solo (because he died; I know there's a new young Han Solo movie coming out but he'll still be dead to me. #Spoiler). For the most part, doing what makes you happy requires a ton of steps to actually get there. And every job is different; therefore, so are the steps to get there. So instead of trying to list all of them, I'm going to boil them down to one step that has made every successful person successful. That step is **work harder.**

Working *harder* is not to be confused with working *hard*. A lot of people work hard. But really successful people work *harder*. Like if you and five other interns are working at a company and four are working hard but only one is working *harder*, that person is going to end up being the other five people's boss.

When I decided that I wanted to be a host and I realized that, unfortunately for me, there was no one wandering the streets looking for a lanky teenage version of Ryan Seacrest, I knew I was going to have to work *harder*. A lot harder. And when I was seventeen, my mom gave me my first opportunity to do that.

As an accountant, my mom handles people's money. So when a production company owed her money, she told them that wouldn't take them to court, as long as they put her son (me) on their next production as an intern. And in fear of my mom financially ruining them, they hired me!

I was fresh out of high school, and it was my first time ever being on a REAL TV SET! Well, not really a *set*. And not really *TV*. And not even really *real*. They had hired me on a low-budget web series that was shooting at a public park in Inglewood, California. The workdays were at a minimum eighteen hours long for seven days straight, and I'm not kidding when I say someone was murdered at that park a few nights before we started. After full days of standing and running and standing again, my feet felt like they were on fire, I got yelled at relentlessly for getting coffee orders wrong, and honestly, I loved every second of it!

For some reason, I actually loved working *harder* than I ever had before. And as an intern, you inevitably work *much harder* than anyone else on set because you're at the bottom of the chain. But after every four-hour night of sleep, I again woke up excited to mess up people's coffee orders!

I made as many contacts as I could that week, which led to job after job in the industry as a production assistant, office runner, grip, gaff, assistant camera operator, everything! I was obsessed with working harder because I was finally doing something I loved way more than my job at Starbucks . . . which, ironically, still revolved around making people's coffee, but that's beside the point.

This was all happening while I was struggling through community college and starting my own YouTube channel. I had made videos for school projects, *most of which I pray you never see*, but I was finally ready to start producing videos for the world. So like everyone else, I started with a vlog, which I deleted. Then I put together a video about dating cougars, which I privated . . . *because it was a video about me dating cougars*. The next video I uploaded and deleted was shot with my friend Sam during the Stuff Girls Say trend that happened in 2010. Being from the Valley, I impersonated a Valley girl in our version, and it ended up being my first viral video. Then the best thing in the world happened: girls started recognizing me as the "Valley Girl." In hindsight it sounds weird that I was recognized for how I looked in a wig and bikini, but at the time it was incredible. There was also one more person who noticed the video, and it landed me the best job ever.

Sam's older brother Josh had seen our simple video online and thought I would make for a perfect addition to the start-up where he had just begun working. He explained to me that the company was small, and very new, but they were focusing on YouTube and paying people to make videos.

This is perfect, I thought. A place that paid people to make YouTube videos? That video I did about Valley girls got over a hundred thousand views and I made exactly zero dollars from it. *But this place would've paid me!* I thought, *They need me. I have one semi-viral video and* **two hundred subscribers.** *I'm basically the next Tyler Oakley.*

So I planned out this fifteen-thousand-dollar travel show where me and a few friends would go from one of end of the country to the other . . . and then go back. *I was going to get those suckers to pay for me to have fun.* I printed out multiple copies of the budget and one sheet, put them in my bag, and went to my first interview. After a thirty-minute conversation, they hired me as an *unpaid intern.* No budget or one-sheet needed.

Okay, so not exactly a cross-country payday, but at least I was working in the field I was interested in! My mom agreed to support me financially for two months of the internship before I'd have to get a real job, and that is how I started at AwesomenessTV.

This was **not** the same AwesomenessTV you know and love today. When I started, Awe-somenessTV was just figuring out what they needed to do to reach a younger audience, and I thought I was the perfect man for the job. On my second day there, I went to the first ever shoot of a makeover show called *Make Me Over,* and the small but up-and-coming YouTuber hosting it was a lady by the name of Bethany Mota.

In the early morning I prepared for my day of coffee fetching and paperwork organizing, but quickly wanted to ask my supervisor something.

> *Hunter: Scotty, does anyone shoot behind the scenes of this?*
> *Scotty: No, but the bosses have talked about doing it one day.*
> *Hunter: Well, I brought all my camera gear, I can shoot it if you'd like . . .*
> *Scotty: . . . Okay, but you still have to get me coffee.*

Did I totally plan that conversation and moment out the night before the shoot? *Maybe.*

Either way, I shot the piece, edited it together, and delivered it to Scotty before the end of the week. He watched it with the normal kind of annoyed look he always has on his face, then said he needed to show someone else. So he walked up to the FOUNDERS OF THE COMPANY and had me hold the computer out for them to watch. I was freaking out. It was five minutes of emotional pain, and like two minutes of my arms being pretty tired from holding the computer. After it finished, they asked me who I was, and I told them I was an intern.

They said, *not anymore*. And right then and there I became an employee of AwesomenessTV. My mom had given me two months to get a job; well, I did it in less than one week because I worked *harder*. All that time I had spent on set learning from high-budget crews, and the time I had spent producing my own low-budget videos, made me the perfect puzzle piece for AwesomenessTV. I accomplished my first goal, but my next would prove to be a little harder. *I wanted to become the face of the company.*

I knew the bosses were watching, so I would make sure to be the first one in the door every day, 7:45 a.m., and the last one out, 8:30 p.m. I also made sure to sit in a place the bosses could see when they walked in an hour after me. The hours spent in the office, plus my one-hour commute to and from work each way, took up every ounce of my time, and they noticed.

After producing and writing projects for Tiffany Alvord, JennXPenn, Andrea Russett, Lia Marie Johnson, and more, I started to get a little antsy. Don't get me wrong, I loved what I was doing and the people I was filming, but I wanted desperately to be on the *other* side of that camera. So after months of producing videos, I straight-up told my bosses that they were wasting their money with me if they weren't going to put me in front of the camera . . . which, looking back, was an incredibly risky thing to do, but it actually paid off.

They put me in charge of writing, shooting, editing, and most important, *hosting* a daily Hollywood news show. That show ended up being the *Daily Report*, and I've now hosted over one thousand episodes of it.

From there I went on to host a number of other Awesomeness shows, including *IMO*, *#DearHunter*, *Third Wheel*, *Do It for the Dough*, and a huge daily show called *Top Five Live*. It's led to me interviewing big stars on every red carpet known to man. It's granted me the opportunity to work with some of the biggest producers in the industry. But most important, it's made me happy, and it's all because I worked *harder*.

FRIENDSHIP
FAMILY L♡VE
SCHOOL
HEARTBREAK
hustles

7

INSECURITIES
STRUGGLES

> Sorry. I'm having a moment. I need some body positivity in my life rn. What's your fave part of your body?

Lauren Elizabeth: I like that I have really big eyes. 🥺

Claudia Sulewski: I really like my little button nose. Is that strange? Probably.

Andrew Lowe: Not strange. My nose too. Love my nose. I don't know why, I just I think it's a good nose. It's defined. It's nice. It's like a solid nose.

Alex Aiono: I love my smile. It's not perfect, but I always have it on!

Maddy Whitby: Same here. I'm chill with my smile. After seven years of braces I better be chill with my smile.

> SEVEN YEARS?!

Monica Sherer: I actually really like my small boobs now. I think I like them because I used to hate them and I've learned to just own it.

Ryan Abe: I like my triceps. I work hard on them. They take up most of your shirt; if you have big triceps you can trick people into thinking you have bigger biceps.

Veronica Merrell: My tiny hands and wrists. I can fit my hand inside of a Pringles can.

> Veronica, you are the chosen one. 🙏

Katherine Cimorelli: I like how tall I am!

Amy Cimorelli: Haha, I like how short I am!

Dani Cimorelli: I like my whole face a lot; tbh I'm cute as heck.

> I FEEL SO MUCH BETTER! I love myself and my gigantic mouth. Thanks everyone.

What do you love about yourself?
Tweet me @HunterMarch with #TBHILoveMy

The Lion in the Mirror

When I was in elementary and middle school, I never really thought about my body. I mean, I knew that I was *the skinny kid*, but all that meant was that I had a six-pack without ever having to work for it. And because I already had what my classmates wanted, I never worried about my body.

But then I graduated, went to high school, and everything changed. All of a sudden my underdeveloped six-pack was being overshadowed by high school sophomores (who looked like college seniors) who had eight-packs. And unlike me, they also had things called *biceps*, and *triceps*, and other *ceps* that I didn't even know existed! When I looked at myself, I saw my arms as spaghetti, and my legs as angel hair pasta. Meanwhile the guys in my class had overstuffed raviolis on their chests and meatballs for biceps. That's when, for the first time, I realized I was the skinniest person in the room, and that included the girls. Well, the skinniest aside from my brother, Dylan. Being a twig runs in the family, and let's just say it *sprints* with him.

I tried
everything.

Now, I know what you're thinking: *But being skinny is great!* Sure, as long as you're healthy, *skinny* is at the top of many people's physical goals. The problem was, I didn't *want* to be skinny. Just like the media promotes being tall and thin, the media also makes us guys think that we have to be toned, muscular, and weirdly tan. It may not be the same intense pressure that women experience, but we still feel it. And because I felt that pressure, I decided I wanted to change my body.

Throughout all four years of high school, I tried everything. First it was protein shakes. I don't know if you've ever had a protein shake, but it tastes like a combination of chocolate and sand. I spent fifty dollars on a bag of it, and drank it twice a day, for half of one day, then I threw it out.

Then I realized that I never ate as much as the guys I wanted to look like. I rarely ever even finished a full plate of food. I would get two-thirds through a meal and then save the rest for later, which is extremely *cost* effective, but not *gains* effective. So I ate until I wanted to throw up for about a week, then I did throw up, and I stopped doing that.

After that short stint of trial and error, I essentially gave up for the remainder of high school. I was okay being the *skinny kid* . . .

AND THEN DYLAN GOT HUGE.

That's right, my little brother, who had always been a skinnier version of my already skinny self, had gone away to college, started teaching gymnastics during the day, taking Muay Thai fighting classes at night, and eating enough food to keep a small elephant content. Basically he lived and breathed fitness and for months, he just kept growing. He went from 140 pounds his sophomore year of college to almost 180 pounds by the time he graduated. You know that picture with the kitten looking into the mirror and seeing a lion? Well, Dylan was the lion, and I was a skinnier version of the kitten.

So I started calling him every day, pretending I cared about his career choices and life dilemmas, all to ask him about how he went from a tree branch to an entire forest.

He told me that he was working out for at least two hours every day between his job as a gymnastics coach and his after-school weight lifting. Personally, I was clocking in close to two hours a month at that point. He told me about his thousand-calorie protein shakes that he was drinking when he woke up and when he went to bed. And he told me about the meals he was eating: chicken, rice, and vegetables, six times a day.

I was immediately motivated and started doing exactly what he was telling me, but the results just weren't coming in. Sure, I put on a couple of pounds. I went from a guy with no pecs to a guy who *almost* had pecs, but I was no lion. Between my almost sixty hours a week working at AwesomenessTV and the countless hours I spent on my YouTube channel, I just couldn't commit the time necessary to have the body I *really* wanted. The body that would make me happy.

I knew that I shouldn't have cared as much, but it's not always easy to love your body, especially in the entertainment industry. I once went through weeks of auditioning for a part that I ultimately didn't get because I was too small compared to my female cohost. I've interviewed guys for AwesomenessTV who make me look like I'm still in middle school. Heck, I've even interviewed middle schoolers who intimidate me. And yes, sometimes that got to me.

Looking back, I was treating my body like it was some sort of accessory; like a used back-pack that I wanted to replace with a newer, bigger backpack. A backpack with *quadriceps* and *quinticeps* and *quantumceps*. But then it hit me. My body isn't an accessory, my body

Every single one of us is someone's definition of perfect.

is me, and it's the only one I'll ever have. I realized that I didn't need to change my *body* to be happy, I needed to change my *relationship with* my body. Sure, I'd still work out and become stronger, but I had to accept that I was never going to look like Dwayne "The Rock" Johnson. My body was always going to look like, well, me. Like a Dwayne "The Pebble" Johnson.

Loving your body is loving yourself, and loving yourself makes you so much more attractive. Because you know what literally EVERYONE IN THE ENTIRE UNIVERSE thinks is hot? Confidence!

There is no *perfect* body. There is no magic number on the scale that makes any one person better than anyone else. There is no *one* definition of beautiful or attractive, because looks are completely subjective. There is someone out there, looking for you right now. Every single one of us is someone's definition of perfect.

Anyway, do I think lions are awesome? Yes. But I like being a kitten; they're cute, and *waaay* better to cuddle with.

Puberty Fails

Puberty is awkward, and that awkwardness is only compounded by the fact that it happens during the most judgmental part of one's life. High school. Well, high school for me. Middle school for others, college for some, but the bottom line is everyone experiences it and it's never flawless. There are some perks, like short people get taller, muscles start appearing, and girl friends sometime become girlfriends. But those great things are often outweighed by the puberty demons that wait until your most vulnerable, public moment to rear their acne-filled faces. These are those stories.

(PS Since there are certain aspects of puberty I can't speak to because I'm not a girl, I've also asked MadMoni, aka Maddy Whitby and Monica Sherer, to help me out with some puberty nightmares of their own.)

MUSTACHE? MUST NOT.

When I was in ninth grade, all I wanted was to be able to grow a mustache. Imagine how good I would've looked: a thick mustache crawling across my lip, right above my braces-filled mouth . . . Okay, looking back, that's gross, but for Christmas that year, I asked Santa for that *sweeeet* lip sweater. That's how bad I wanted it, but ninth grade passed, and alas, I had no 'stache.

Tenth grade, nothing.

Eleventh grade, still nothing.

Finally, it was my senior year, and no change. Then, after a soccer practice with my team where I swear I was the only one without a mustache, we went back to the locker room. In the middle of changing, a teammate yelled, "Whoa! Hunter with the hair!"

I'VE DONE IT! I thought. I have facial hair and they are the first to notice it!

When I turned, though, they weren't pointing at my face. Their fingers were aimed directly . . . at my butt. I looked down and for the first time noticed where all the hair I had wished for had gone. Thanks, Santa. My butt now had a permanent cardigan.

CRACKING UP CRACKS 'EM UP

Another terrible side effect of becoming an adult is the voice change. What makes it terrible is that it doesn't happen all at once, like a snake shedding its skin. Instead it drags on forever, like a snake trying to shed its skin, except it keeps getting caught on things, and all of that snake's middle school peers keep calling him out, but it's not the snake's fault, all snakes shed their skin, ALL SNAKES SHED THEIR SKIN!

Basically, as a person's voice changes, the new, deeper adult voice is constantly fighting with the kid voice, and everyone can see the fight. That's the voice crack.

I remember having to give a speech in my English class in front of "*Monika*," my crush. All I could do was pray that my voice didn't crack. So what did my voice do? It cracked. *It cracked hard*. It cracked like a lightbulb being dropped from an airplane. And once it started cracking, it didn't stop. It was like my body's way of reminding me that I'd never be cool. I could've been delivering the best speech ever, the Gettysburg Address of middle school speeches, but all I would ever be remembered for was my voice cracking . . . *If we're being honest, though, I probably wrote that speech the night before. Sorry for comparing myself to you, Abe.*

STUDY HALL, MORE LIKE STUDY *BRA* (HAHA)
Monica Sherer

I am and always have been president of the Itty Bitty Titty Committee. And I'm fine with that . . . now. However, that wasn't always the case.

I remember when I was in sixth grade and all of the girls were getting boobs and there was this kid in my study hall who would always snap girls' bras as a "prank." Being the tiny, flat-chested teen that I was, I didn't wear a bra yet, and it became my recurring nightmare that he would one day try to snap my bra and announce to the world that I wasn't wearing one, thus drawing attention to my lack of boob, thus causing the *ultimate humiliation*. Finally, it became such a real fear that I made my mom take me to Kohl's and I BOUGHT A BRA. That's right, I only started wearing bras *out of fear* that a stupid boy in study hall wouldn't snap it.

I can't remember if he ever did, but I can honestly say that I wore bras more frequently in middle school and high school than I do today. #BOOBLESSANDPROUD

A TERRIBLE, HORRIBLE, NO GOOD, VERY BAD PERIOD STORY.
Maddy Whitby

I got my period super late compared to most girls. Really late. Like, *seventeen* years old late. *So* late that when it finally came, I thought I was completely prepared! I had heard all of my other friends' period horror stories, and read the tampon pamphlet front to back (do other people do that?). Turns out, your first period isn't always what you expect, no matter how ready you *think* you are. The story starts in my dorm room on a cold December night in northern Michigan . . .

I was lucky enough to go to a boarding high school for the arts (like real-life *Zoey 101*, but in the middle of the stupidly cold forest). Now, they say that periods always come at the most inconvenient times, so it was only right that it *finally* decided to show up during FINALS WEEK. Ugh. I tried to keep my chill, using that tampon pamphlet every time I got confused or scared I wasn't doing it right (yes, that's the second time I've said "tampon pamphlet." That's the third), and was doing just fine! Until the fifth day. I was so stressed out with periods and finals, I didn't think it could get any worse. Just as I was finishing a fifteen-page essay on *Jane Eyre*, I suddenly got the *worst* nosebleed of ALL TIME. Such an aggressive/violent/Niagara-esque nosebleed all over my favorite uniform shirt. After that, I just remember lying on the floor of my dorm room, tampons sticking out of both nostrils, screaming, "THERE'S BLOOD EVERYWHERE!!!"

Every period after that felt like a Playtex commercial in a pair of white linen pants. My mom ended up sending me newer, better, less bloody uniform shirts, and I finally learned how to use a tampon without the tampon pamphlet (that makes four times). Tampon pamphlet, tampon pamphlet, tampon pamphlet.

IS IT NIPPY IN HERE?

Everything Monica, Maddy, and I have mentioned above was awkward and embarrassing, but I always felt okay about it because other people were going through it with me. That was, except for one thing.

One day, during my puberty adventure, my nipples felt super tender . . . that last sentence is so weird, I apologize, but it's true. Over the next couple of months, they also became, for lack of a better word, puffier.

It was, and probably still is, what I'm most self-conscious of on my body. Unlike the pathetic mustaches, and the high-pitched voice cracks, I seemed to be the only one in my school dealing with this. Thin shirts became unwearable, going to pools seemed like a nightmare, and my brother thought it was the funniest thing ever. I held back tears telling my parents how much I hated my nipples (again a weird sentence) but they told me the puffiness would go away. Unfortunately, though, it never did.

Instead I started working out, naturally grew a little taller and bigger, and they seemed less apparent on my body. I still noticed them, but I stopped letting them control my life. It wasn't until years later that a YouTuber I was friends with uploaded a video talking about having the same issue. That one video made me feel one thousand times better about them. In fact, I feel so good that I could literally shout, "I LOVE MY PUFFY NIPPLES!"

But I won't, 'cause that's another weird sentence.

Some people are early bloomers and get facial hair or boobs in the fifth grade. Others, like me, are late bloomers and still can't really grow a mustache, and honestly my voice cracked reading this chapter aloud to my girlfriend.

The silver lining is that no matter what pace you're going through it, EVERYONE is going through, or has gone through, the exact same thing. Even the things you think are just affecting you alone are affecting other people as well. So while everything that is happening may FEEL embarrassing, it isn't. It's just a part of life.

Why I Don't Wear Short Shorts

Andrew Lowe

Growing up, I thought eating disorders were for girls. On TV shows and in advertisements, the media tended to portray struggling with body image as a feminine issue; something *girls* go through. So when I started struggling with my own body image, I kept it a secret. I thought, *This isn't an experience for boys.*

I remember the exact moment it began. I had just finished third grade and my family and I were on a summer road trip. To pass the time in the car, I was going through pictures from the year. Picture by picture, I started to realize that throughout the year I had gained some weight. Not too much, but enough to make me immediately start crying. I was so ashamed. Not just because I had gotten a little chubby, but because I thought boys weren't supposed to care about that kind of thing, yet there I was crying about it. I was ashamed of being ashamed. Naturally, as any parent would do if their child randomly broke out into tears, my moms asked me what was wrong. I didn't want to tell the truth, so I lied and said I was crying because I was going to miss school during summer break. *What type of kid cries because school ends?* I don't know, but they believed me, and I had successfully suppressed my feelings for the first time. Hooray! That was the beginning.

I continued to gain weight, and then throughout fourth and fifth grade I got bullied about it. Not a lot, but every now and then someone would just be like, "You're fat" and I would be like, "Um, okay" and then go cry about it. I was constantly comparing my body to those of the other boys in my class. When I got to middle school and we were required to change clothes for gym, the self-comparison just got worse. I felt like everyone was skinnier than me, and the thought of getting undressed in front of the other guys was so terrible that it made math class seem like a good time.

Seventh grade was when I started trying to do things about it. Since I still held the notion that guys weren't supposed to care how they looked, I felt the need to keep my efforts a secret. I would go so far as to pretend I was sick just so I could stay home from school to watch eight-minute ab videos and go on runs while my parents were gone. But that only got me so far.

Starting sometime in eighth grade I basically *stopped* eating. It wasn't immediate; I was back and forth a lot. Eating one day and then not eating another. Eating and then making myself throw up. But eventually I was just not eating. Since I didn't want anyone to know, I started coming up with tricks. In the morning I would take breakfast with me and say I was going to eat it on the bus, and then I just wouldn't. My mom would make lunches for me and once I got to school I would throw them away. Dinner was harder to get out of. Sometimes I would say I had a ton of homework and needed to eat in my bedroom, only to flush it down the toilet or give it to my dog.

I never said out loud, *I have an eating disorder*. But I knew what it was. I had tried to eat healthy, but since I was a kid I didn't have much control over what I was eating. My mom made my lunch and my parents cooked dinner every night. I felt like I couldn't eat as

I struggled for so long.

healthy as I wanted and I was too embarrassed to show that I cared, so I just didn't eat. I knew not eating was bad. But I also felt like it was working. The hunger started to feel good.

Then, since it turns out your body needs food to, like, live and stuff, I became pretty ill after a while. My immune system started deteriorating and I stayed sick most of eighth grade. There was a solid eight-month period where I was in and out of the doctor's office every few weeks. Since I had done a pretty good job of hiding my eating habits, no doctor could really figure out what was wrong with me. They'd diagnose me with something random and give me medication for it—but it would obviously never work.

I knew what was wrong with me, but I wasn't concerned about my health. I was more worried about getting caught. Sometimes I'd get scared someone would notice the weight loss and ask me about it, so I'd then binge eat in attempts to gain some back. I'd also do that when I knew I had a doctor's appointment coming up where I knew my weight would be checked. Then I'd hate myself for doing that, so I'd stop eating again. That's one of the reasons I think I struggled for so long. The cycle of starving and then binging and then starving probably made it last longer than it could have.

I don't want to say I was depressed because, like, I don't know. But I did get pretty bummed about my existence. It took a toll on me, and it led to me feeling a lot of guilt. My family wasn't the richest, so watching my moms pay for all the doctor visits and unnecessary medications only added to the guilt I felt from throwing food away. I hated my body and hated what I was doing and was just pretty miserable. I remember thinking *I am killing my body* because of it, yet I didn't care. At the time I would've rather been dead than alive and fat.

Eventually a friend caught on. He gradually noticed that I wasn't really eating at lunch or when we'd hang out. While it felt sort of comfortable having someone know without having to say it out loud, my habit was just getting worse. There'd be days near the end of it all that I'd wake up and not even be able to sit up without passing out. I wasn't present in my life. So much energy was devoted to not eating, it was like I wasn't really there.

This has to end now.

One day that friend and I were in gym together and I got called to the counselor's office without any idea why. When I got there we made casual conversation for a while, but our chat about the weather abruptly ended when she dropped something along the lines of "So your friend tells me you don't eat a lot, what's up with that?" I was so uncomfortable and so embarrassed, and so mad at my friend for telling someone. I didn't talk to him for a week. He was just, you know, trying to keep his best friend alive, yet I was livid.

The counselor called home and that was when my parents first found out. I avoided them when I got home from school so we didn't talk much about it. But I knew they knew some-thing, and it was in that moment that, more than ever, I thought, *This has to end now.*

It didn't really end, though. That's the thing with eating disorders: they don't really end. They kind of just become inactive. I started eating normally again, but the self-hatred and instincts to eat less still followed me. I may have been healthier, but it felt like giving up. It felt like I was going to be fat for the rest of my life and that was that.

Once I got to high school I noticed that all the guys around me finally started to care about how they looked. Everyone wanted abs and arms and girls, so people started getting gym memberships. Being the violently insecure person I was, I had no desire to join a public gym, where I'd be surrounded by hot people and risk the chance of seeing someone I knew. How-ever, I definitely had the desire to throw my husky-fit jeans away and stop hating myself.

We had this sad room in our basement that had no windows and always smelled like a combination of cat food and cat poop. What it did have was a stationary bike in the corner that no one used. That stationary bike was my beacon of hope. Every day for over a year I'd come home from school, change into gym clothes, go to the basement, lock the door, put my earphones in, and blast Katy Perry pump-up jams while I rode the bike for half an hour. Every day. I'm not even a big Katy Perry fan, but *Prism* came out around the same time I started and somehow became the soundtrack of this ritual. I now know every word to every song on *Prism*, and truly owe Katy props for at least thirty pounds of my weight loss. If you're reading this, Katy, thanks for the bops! "Roar" still gets me goin'.

Eventually, I got more confident with my body. Don't get me wrong, I didn't *and still don't* wear tank tops in public, but I started wearing shorts! That sounds like a mild milestone, but previously I hated my legs so much that I was dedicated to wearing jeans even if it was a hundred degrees and humid. I always felt like I had full-grown cows, not calves, so being comfortable enough with my legs to wear shorts was a big deal. It was around this time that I started to have a prominent online presence, so I'd sometimes tweet weight loss milestones and people would cheer me on. It was great! Maybe I wasn't going to be fat and sad for the rest of my life after all!

I see a personal trainer now that I live in LA, and it's all about strength training. So I'm not really trying to lose weight; it's about being stronger. However, to build and maintain muscle I have to eat more than I'm used to and I'm not going to lie, the instincts still kick in. I constantly think, *Whoa, I'm eating a lot. Slow down, Monsters, Inc.* graduate. It's still a part of my life. I'm constantly concerned about what I'm eating and how my body looks, but it's a process.

The biggest change is that the shame is gone. I'm not sporting short shorts every day, I'm not wearing tank tops in public, I'm definitely not sitting down while shirtless, and I still sometimes "forget" my swimsuit at home during beach trips. I don't necessarily love my body, but I don't hate it anymore either. And that's a step in the right direction. That extra layer of shame is gone, too. I know now that everyone, girls *and* guys, struggles with body image growing up. It's not a rare thing. It's not just a female thing. It sucks, but it's normal to have things that make you feel bad about yourself. However it doesn't help to not say anything. I think if I had talked to my friends, if I had told my parents, if I had been more open about my eating disorder struggles, I might have gotten over the bad part sooner.

Hopefully one day I'll reach a place where I feel totally comfortable with my body; it's just a journey. I'd love to get to a place where I learn to love my body as it is; I just haven't learned how to yet. *Does anyone know that secret?* If anyone does know, please tell me. That sounds a lot easier than working out.

That's the reason why I haven't been really open about it on the internet. When people notice my weight loss success and then come to me for advice on body image, I have no idea what to say. If you're asking for help, you're already a step ahead of where I was. I just don't feel like I have the advice for loving yourself. I wish I did, but what I do now know is that it's okay not to. Everyone struggles growing up, and that's okay! Even if you're a boy in third grade and you think you're fat! I'm still working on feeling better about myself. I don't have it all figured out, but I don't think anyone does.

My Armor

Meghan Tonjes

What is the hardest thing you've been through?

For me, the answer is simple.

Middle school.

Middle school was the height of my awkward phase.

I was a clear foot taller and at least fifty pounds heavier than any of my friends, and my *differences* felt more pronounced; figuratively and literally, I took up more space.

I wasn't a stranger to having the occasional "fat" whispered at me in the hallway, but had been able to brush most of them off. Maybe that word was for someone else, missing its intended target. Maybe I had misheard.

It wasn't until the end of sixth grade that I became fully aware. Not only was I fat, but also the world saw it and had no problem reminding me. I remember the moment it started to feel like I had a big scarlet *F* etched onto my chest.

We used to have these school dances. Parents would drop students off at the school gymnasium for a few hours of candy, pizza, and awkward hands-on-shoulders dancing.

When I was twelve years old, I officially went to my first dance. Wearing an ill-fitting striped sweater dress, I decided to focus more on the candy and pizza than the dancing. To be fair, most of the night had been spent with a group of boys tormenting me. One by one they would come up to me, telling me that their mutual friend wanted to ask for a dance; that he liked me. It didn't take long for me to realize these boys were playing a joke on their friend . . . a classic game of Make the Fat Girl Think You Like Her.

Don't cry in front of them. This was my mantra at the time.

Don't cry in front of them.

So, as the last song played, I sat on a bench finishing my last dollar slice of pizza.

And, as I got up to throw my napkin away, two older girls approached me. I knew they were eighth graders, but couldn't quite remember their names. I still don't remember their names.

"We wanted to ask you something!"

"Okay . . . what is it?"

"We heard a rumor and wanted to see if it's true. Are you pregnant?"

— ⬤ —

Looking back, I wish I had planned some sort of snarky comeback. Something pithy and brilliant. Instead, I squeaked a quiet no and pushed past them to throw out my trash. I can still hear their muffled laughs; see the huge smiles on their faces as they left me completely deflated.

Don't cry in front of them.

And I didn't.

It wasn't until I got in the passenger side of my mom's car that I broke down in sobs.

And through the tears and deep gasps for air, I was just barely able to put what had happened into words.

I expected my mom to look at me and tell me I was perfect, that I was beautiful and nothing those girls said mattered.

Instead, she cleared her throat and simply said, "Meghan. With the way you look, people are going to say those things."

—— ● ——

The world couldn't have seemed lonelier than it did in that moment. I felt betrayed. I felt angry. I felt like I had been cheated out of something. Granted, if my mom had said, "You're perfect!", I probably wouldn't have listened to her at all. Still, it wasn't what I wanted or expected to hear.

Now, this is where the story becomes something I'm not really proud of.

Because for the next fifteen years I carried those words with me. I let them grow into an unspoken anger, a beneath-the-surface resentment that fueled any and all fights I had with my mom. If we couldn't see eye to eye, it wasn't because she didn't like my haircut or one of my friends. For me, it was because of what she had said all those years ago.

—— ● ——

Part of growing up is about going back through the big moments of your life, breaking them down and really trying to see them with fresh eyes. As I started to unpack parts of myself, I always came back to these words.

With the way you look, people are going to say those things.

But something started to happen the older I got. I stopped feeling the same. When I retold the story, I didn't feel that old anger or sadness.

The words didn't hurt me anymore. In fact, they started to make sense.

So much of what I had done in YouTube and music had been centered around the idea of acknowledging how the world saw me and breaking those assumptions. I openly called myself fat. I worked, wrote, and toured so I could prove that someone like me COULD be successful as a musician. I started a collab channel, Project Lifesize, because I demanded to have real conversations about body image, find connection to others who had felt similar pressures to look a certain way. In every way my life centered around being visible and unapologetic.

And here I was, being haunted by something I already knew. With the way I looked, people were going to say those things. People loved saying "those things." But "those things" didn't have the same power they'd once had.

Instead of feeling betrayed or abandoned, I started to see what my mom said for what it really was. She had told me the truth, in all of its unrefined sharpness. She had tried to prepare me for a world that wasn't always going to be kind. Who I am isn't always going to line up with how others see me.

That's okay.

When you know how the world sees you, there are no more secrets. You're free to stay in that box or completely tear the box down.

Yes, with the way I look, people are going to talk. So what? Is that the worst thing? If anything, I'd love to give them something to talk about. I want them to see me so they can't deny my strength or my accomplishments. Is the word *fat* really the worst thing someone can say about me? That word has as much power as I give it. And if someone is using fat to mean lazy, ugly, unaccomplished, unlovable, let me prove them wrong by existing in my truth, by exceeding their expectations and simply meeting my own. Sometimes the things that make you feel the weakest, that hurt you the most, become part of your defense.

When I was twelve, my mother gave me a gift that I didn't understand or appreciate until I needed it the most.

My armor.

Be honest! What is the most embarrassing thing that has ever happened to you?

Lauren Elizabeth
One time in history class I threw up on a girl's feet. Everyone found out during the pep rally later that day and started laughing at me. I'm talking THE ENTIRE SCHOOL.

Amy Cimorelli
A guy sent me a selfie. I wanted to send it to my friend to show her how cute he was, and I accidentally sent it to HIM. Literally, I sent him A PICTURE OF HIM and said "JFSJDK-SKDKSK." It was awful.

Lauren Cimorelli
At VidCon I leaned against a wall, only it wasn't a wall. It was a sign, and I fell over and broke the sign too . . .

Andrew Lowe
Mine was when I 💩 my pants in elementary school. My friends dared me to do a backflip over a bar thing. I was so nervous that when I did the backflip I 💩 my pants. I did a back 💩.

LOLOLOL.

Maddy Whitby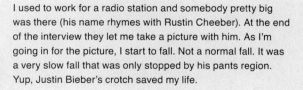
I used to work for a radio station and somebody pretty big was there (his name rhymes with Rustin Cheeber). At the end of the interview they let me take a picture with him. As I'm going in for the picture, I start to fall. Not a normal fall. It was a very slow fall that was only stopped by his pants region. Yup, Justin Bieber's crotch saved my life.

Meg DeAngelis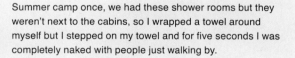
Summer camp once, we had these shower rooms but they weren't next to the cabins, so I wrapped a towel around myself but I stepped on my towel and for five seconds I was completely naked with people just walking by.

Vanessa Merrell
In kindergarten, I was pantsed by a boy! It scarred me for life.

Ouch. I got a pantsing story for you, hold on to your . . . pants.

Tell me your embarrassing stories!
Tweet me @HunterMarch with **#TBHSoEmbarrassing**

The Upside-Down Pantsing

We all have embarrassing moments in our lives. Some happen in front of your crush. Some seem to go on forever. And others end with everyone seeing your wiener. My story involves all three.

I was in sixth grade. An absolutely horrible time in my life, but that was about to change. We were graduating that week, and seventh grade was just around the corner. Freedom.

But before that, my family and some family friends were going to go on our first summer trip of the year. Per tradition, we would all pile into multiple SUVs with boats in tow and drive four hours north away from Los Angeles to Bass Lake. I LOVED these trips. I got to hang out with my cousins from San Diego, *not* do homework, and most important, cheerleaders were going to be there.

One of our family friends had a daughter on the high school cheerleading team, and *by the grace of God*, she brought five of her cheerleader friends with her on our vacation. This was literally like five of my dreams coming true at once. I knew once they saw me do my famous dolphin dive into the lake, they would all fall in love and I'd be forced to choose but I wouldn't be able to and we'd all get married after I graduated . . . middle school.

The excitement was almost too much to handle. Actually, it was too much to handle. I was notorious for being an awful car mate at that time in my life, but this trip was worse than ever. I incorrectly sang the lyrics to every song that came on the radio and had to pee every ten miles. Dads hate that. *I don't know if anyone else noticed this, but dads have camel bladders. I'm positive.*

The excitement was almost too much to handle.

Anyway. That year my uncle Rob drew the short stick when I decided to ride with my cousins in his car. Let me tell you about Uncle Rob: He doesn't like singing even when the lyrics are correct, he thinks bathroom breaks are a waste of time, and he despises having grapes thrown at the back of his head. *How did I find that last one out, you ask?*

I was throwing grapes at the back of my uncle's head from the moment we left Los Angeles. I don't know what it was about his head, but it was so big, with this perfect target of where hair *used* to be, and I was a sniper. I'd eat one, then toss one to Uncle Rob for him to eat one. Except he was never looking because he was driving and it would just hit him in that sweet, sweet cranium. I went through about thirty grapes that way until he did one of those *adult car-turn-arounds* and said, *If you throw one more grape up here you're going to regret it!*

I had never seen him so angry. His face was almost as red as the spot on his head where I had continually pelted him with grapes. I sank, and immediately regretted all the grapes I had thrown. I told myself to stop . . . but then I noticed I was holding the heaviest grape in all the bag. He was in my hand, looking up at me, begging me in a little grape voice to let him fly like his brothers and sisters had. *How could I deny him?*

I launched the grape and it landed smack dab in the middle of his male pattern baldness, and the second it did, the blinkers went on and the car started to pull over. The cars in the caravan behind us followed suit into a busy gas station.

Everyone stepped out from their cars to stretch or pee (except the dads) and that's when I saw the cheerleaders. They were stretching and it was the greatest thing ever. They were even better than how I described them in that earlier paragraph. I finally understood true love, and I understood it five times over. Nothing in the world could have ruined that mo-ment for—*OH MY GOD, WHY IS UNCLE ROB CHASING ME?!*

Yeah, Uncle Rob was now chasing me around the parking lot and people were starting to watch and laugh. The cheerleaders were laughing, so I even started laughing. Uncle Rob was not laughing. But I was a fast kid and he was a big guy so he would never be able to—*OH MY GOD, HE CAUGHT ME!!*

He swooped me up off the ground and said, "I told you that you'd regret this." Then he turned me upside down and held me by my ankles. Then somehow, *by the grace of the devil*, he reverse-pantsed me. I was hanging upside down with **everything** hanging out. People were hysterical at this point. I locked eyes with my true love, a gaggle of cheerleaders who were all covering their mouths while laughing. I wondered if they were impressed. *Probably not*. It had been kind of chilly in the car.

Finally, my mom pulled into the lot and was not happy with what she saw. She yelled at him to put me down and I scrambled to pull my shorts up, but by then it was too late. They had seen me at my most vulnerable: fully naked while upside down. For the rest of the trip it was very, very awkward.

I didn't end up dating any of them that year, or marrying them after I graduated. I did, though, run into them much later as a twenty-year-old. The daughter of the family friend who brought her cheerleading friends on our trip originally was now getting married and I, along with her same group of cheerleader friends, was going to be in attendance.

For the first time in almost a decade, I would be face-to-face with the first girls to ever see my private parts, and not in a good way. *Would they even remember?* Let me ruin the surprise. They remembered everything.

But this situation is something I've learned so much about over time. Basically it's the famous equation, tragedy + time = comedy. Now obviously some tragedies are just tragic, but others are perfect material for comedy. I've been cheated on, had the worst first kiss of all time, and got the most epic pantsing ever in front of my dream wives. But all of those moments have become incredible stories that I tell time and time again. Eventually everything that happens to you will become a memory that makes you *you*. Just to prove it, when I saw those cheerleaders again, we actually had a huge laugh about the entire situation!

And when I saw them at that wedding, I wasn't the same kid. I was an adult now. More important, I was an adult fully clothed in a suit and tie. And one of those girls who saw *everything* years ago just happened to really like adults in suits and ties. Yep, you know where this is going, I went on a date with one of those cheerleaders not too long after that wedding. Was it all five? No. But you know what they say. Five cheerleaders is a fantasy. One cheerleader is still really cool, though.

Thanks, Uncle Rob.

Screw Adjectives

Alexis G. Zall

Human beings are relatively severely narcissistic. We're obsessed with ourselves. You can see it every time we attempt to determine our personalities via online quizzes, when we display our interests through social media posts, or when we're just at a party with friends, pretending to be the confident one. Personally, I'm the friend who flirts with everyone. I'm the funny friend. I'm the friend who trips often and gives everyone a nice laugh. I've spent a lot of time in my life already trying to be a lot of different adjectives.

When I was younger I was Gymnastics Girl. I didn't *do* gymnastics; I mean, I did, but I wasn't just a girl who did cartwheels for fun after school. I *was* a gymnast. I started when I was twenty-three months old and by the time I was in elementary school, I was training twenty-five to thirty hours a week. It was my life.

But when I started my seventh-grade year, I got injured. Doctors said if I kept working out

I wasn't a gymnast anymore.

the way I was, the muscle of my hamstring would pull away from the bone. Pop clean off, like a confetti cannon or champagne bottle, but significantly less fun. The idea was I would take time off, it would heal, and then I would go back to tumbling passes, talking crap about the chalk bin, and other gymnastics activities. But it didn't heal. And that was just *it*. I wasn't a gymnast anymore.

It was this sudden, weird thing because I had always thought of myself as a gymnast. When I woke up and realized *I am not that person anymore*, I internally FREAKED OUT. But quietly, like when a sinkhole builds underneath a house and you don't know it's there until the whole thing has sunk in one afternoon while you're just out at Costco. I had been so busy I never really thought about whether I liked gymnastics. In hindsight, I didn't so much. I don't think a lot of people consider whether they enjoy brushing their teeth, because it's just something you do. Gymnastics was like that for me. So for the first time in my life, I had this exorbitant amount of free time and it was almost bizarre. I thought, like, *Oh, I can have other interests? That's kind of cool.* But what did humans do if they weren't at the gym or they weren't at school? It was a very big, not so cute question of *Well, if I'm not a gymnast, who am I?*

I started to explore other interests. This may sound kind of weird, but one of the first things I realized was that I loved doing laundry. With my parents paying me to do it, I got to a point where I would tell them, "Change your shirt, I'm going to wash it," because I was so up to date. Then I started gardening. I planted a lot of different things, but the one that really took off was cabbage. I was just like this little kid who had a cabbage patch. Believe me, I get it, I was literally a Cabbage Patch Kid. Then I started screen-printing T-shirts and flipping random things on eBay. I would get trinkets or DVDs at the ninety-nine cent store and sell them on eBay for like three or four dollars to make a tiny profit. I thought, *I'm a goddess of industry, I will own the world.*

But a big part of doing all those things was just to keep busy. I had time to think about things I had never *really* thought about. For example, I spent a lot of time thinking about death. No one around me had died; the reason was more like *I never had time to think about this, so let's do it now.* I had time on time on time for sadness and fear and just general contemplation of the human experience. If you've never thought about your inevitable doom, I wouldn't recommend it. Try reading the whole Harry Potter series or something instead.

In sixth grade I was in a school play and loved it, so I thought I would try out some acting classes. I only started my YouTube channel because I wanted to practice acting, which is not a particularly romantic story; it's kind of the "we met on Tinder" of starting a YouTube channel. Because I didn't see anyone making dramatic three-minute skits, I made comedy videos, even though I'd never thought of myself as a particularly funny person. It took me a while to figure out what I was doing.

If I laughed at a video I watched of another YouTuber, I would watch it over and over to study it. I wanted to know, *When did I laugh? Why did I laugh? What made this funny?* I felt like I was trying to figure out the formula of comedy, like the math behind it, which is definitely the only math I have ever enjoyed doing. I loved this—it all felt very purposeful, the same sort of feeling I'd get when mastering a new gymnastics skill, but somehow better. My friends from gymnastics would sometimes tell me, "I watched a bunch of your videos. They're really funny." So I thought, *I guess this is working.* And it was like I had a new identity.

I was a YouTuber. *Panicked young tween finds herself. She's the "Funny YouTuber Friend."*

Once I was like *I'm a YouTuber,* I started building adjectives on that to have this very specific identity so I could make sure my presence online remained consistent. Cool and confident were kind of my go-tos. I am a YouTuber who is funny, secure, extroverted, and adventurous and totally self-aware. I am a YouTuber who is always looking for a good time and doesn't care what other people think. I really found my voice around my fifteenth birthday. I made a video called "15 Tips for 15 Years." It was one of the first vlog style videos I made. There was something about that video that felt right. It was like *I get it; I see what I'm doing here.* I liked this identity. Who wouldn't want to feel like *I'm cool, I'm fine, and everything is great all the time.*

And then around two years ago I had this weirdly specific identity crisis. My channel is like a log of my life. I had this weird moment where I was like *I have no idea who I am, yet my career is being who I am.* Suddenly I was getting all these, like, totally normal human teenager feelings, and I thought, *Oh no, don't do that. You can't change. You already picked who you are and a lot of people like you as is.* As I grew up I had been changing and evolving as a person and I hadn't really noticed because I had this identity online that stayed the same. Maybe I knew who I was at fourteen, but at sixteen I wasn't fourteen anymore. I had a brand, but I wasn't sure I had an identity. I don't think I was lying about who I was online. Because I had decided I wanted to be all these things. I totally had convinced myself I was. Until I really was not anymore. I struggled for a couple of months and did some of the identity crisis things. Like I got really sad, so I cut off all my hair. It felt right. *Former panicked tween now "cool" and "confident" (yeah right!) teen has classic identity crisis.* In this process I realized a lot of important things.

I have insecurities. Obviously. Everyone has insecurities. To name one of my personal favorites, I am incredibly insecure about my hair. If it isn't exactly how I want it, I think about it constantly. This is something I logically know is very dumb. There are so many more important things in the world, in my life, blah blah blah. But my hair just bothers me. I am not insecure about what other people think of it, I'm insecure if I'm unhappy with it. But if I try to ignore it or tell myself it does not bother me, I'm lying. So I say, *Okay. This is something that is silly but I am insecure about it.* I don't have to try to convince myself to feel otherwise.

I am not always funny. Not everything I do is for comedic entertainment value, which seems obvious. Like, I love quotes. Completely unironically. When I tell people this, sometimes they think I'm joking. I think it is beautiful that someone said something once, and as a collective human force we all decided that was one of the best ways that specific message could be conveyed. *That's not very funny, Alexis, but I guess you're allowed to think that.*

But the biggest realization was that I'm not always a YouTuber, I'm a person. As a YouTuber it sometimes it feels like you have to be "on" all the time. And sometimes I'm just . . . off. Sometimes I get nervous. Which happens. I cannot tackle everything in life with the false stoicism I used to believe I possessed. I used to say "I like everything!" and "It's all good all the time." I used to believe I was impervious to human emotions and always happy and always funny. No one is. That's not real.

So who am I exactly? Who knows. But that is okay, because no teenager or adult or really anyone knows. You change and evolve. Once you figure out who you are, that's already who you *were*. So if you're identity crisis-ing, it's okay. Don't stress over trying to define yourself as a bunch of adjectives. Screw adjectives. *Former panicked tween turned "confident" teen to relatively calm (yet emotional) young adult doesn't stress about definitive identity.* Green with envy, red with rage, blue with sadness, pink with rosy-cheeked happiness, and a smear of maroon because it's my favorite. It all depends on the day. I am a lot of things and I don't need to keep a running tally. I'm here, and I'm trying, and that's enough.

Finding the
Real Me

Rickey Thompson

Growing up I didn't know any gay people. I had seen gay people on TV, mainly when my grandmother would watch *Ellen*, but that was it. Most of what I knew about gay people I learned from a conservative community in Raleigh, North Carolina.

I heard people say being gay was wrong. I heard in school that gay was "bad." I heard that gay people were going to hell. I heard God doesn't approve of gay marriage. I heard if you're gay you can't have a family. *I thought being gay must be awful.*

I was probably around eight or nine when I realized, *oh, this feeling toward guys is so different than what I feel toward girls. Whoa, what is this?* I thought *I'm, like, different but it's just a phase.* So I forced myself to date girls anyway. But freshman year in high school, when I was posing for homecoming pictures with my arms around my girlfriend's waist, I just didn't feel right.

I first admitted it to myself my junior in high school. I said, *Okay, Rickey. you've gone through all these relationships, something is not right. I'm not happy. Am I gay?* I wrote it down to try and make sense of all of it. I wrote, *I am attracted to this, I like this, I'm into this.* When I connected the dots I realized, *Oh, yeah, I am gay.* And when I finally said it to myself, I started to cry.

At this point I had seen more things and had more experiences. I had gay friends on YouTube, so I knew being gay didn't make you bad. I started to realize I could still have a family and just realized, *Oh my family is going to be different, I'm going to have a husband not a wife.* I thought my parents wouldn't understand because my family would be different from theirs and I didn't want them to be disappointed. So I kept it from them.

I kept it from everyone, until I came out to my best friend Kelsey during senior year. She came with me to Playlist Live and there was this guy who kept texting me and I was trying to keep it on the low. Finally, we were partying and I was just like "I have something to tell you, Kelsey. I'm gay." And I started crying. I was so scared because she was the first person I had ever told.

She said, "Boy, it's okay, I know I was just waiting for you to tell me." Her reaction was just perfect. I was so relieved and so happy. She was just like, "That's just who you are attracted to, it doesn't change who you are." Telling Kelsey gave me the courage to tell more people.

So I told all my close internet friends. They were like "Rickey, Congrats, thank you for telling us, that is amazing, it's okay, we love you." After that I started feeling more and confidence in myself. It was like, *I guess I need to start coming out to more and more people.*

Then, when I saw more people accepting me, it was more like, *why I am hiding this when I could be living free?* But I still didn't feel I could come out to my family. I figured it didn't matter; I was graduating and moving to Los Angeles anyway.

But even when I moved to Los Angeles I wasn't really free. When I made videos about crushes, I would say "someone," I would never say "a guy." I wanted to date guys but I was afraid somebody would expose me to the public or to my family at home. I used to be afraid of what other people thought of me. It took me a while but I knew I needed to stop leading a secret life. One day it was just like, *I am this person, and I'm happy about it. Why am I still hiding it?*

I've watched a lot of coming out stories and they have had good or bad outcomes and I don't know why, but I thought I would be someone who had the bad one. My best friend Anthony was just like, "you should just let people know, who cares?"

So I tweeted out "I'm over hiding it, I like guys." It was simple—nothing big, nothing too emotional. I was just like, *This is who I am.* When I first tweeted it, I was really nervous but more than that, I was relieved. In that moment I didn't care what anybody thought about me. I got so many positive responses that I cried for the longest time. I just kept looking at tweet after tweet and crying. The outpouring of support was incredible. I kept thinking, *I'm in the light now, you guys.* I couldn't stop saying, "I'm so, so happy."

Then I got a call from my mother. My father is a barber and one of his customers came in and said, "Congratulations to your son," and showed him the tweet. He was highly confused and he told my mother. She was like, "Hello, Rickey, how are you, did you tweet something?" I knew exactly what she was talking about. I was like, *Ohmigod.* I wasn't ready. So I just blurted it out, "yeah, Mom, I'm gay."

I was sure I knew how she was going to react. I thought my family would disown me. That's why when things happened in my life, I turned to my camera and not to my family. I just felt comfortable putting my life out there to them because thousands and thousands of people were always welcoming me. But even if they didn't accept me, I didn't have to go home to them.

But my family was my home. To my complete surprise she said, "Sweetie, I always knew you were different and I love you but it hurts me that you came out to the public before you came out to your family." She wasn't upset that I was gay, she was upset that I didn't feel like I could tell her. Thinking about it now, I get it. If I was a parent and I heard some random person said, "Did you hear this information about your son?" I would be hurt too.

All the women in my family reacted like my mom. They were all basically like, "we knew, boo." My dad didn't say that. He didn't know. He wasn't sure how to react. He sent me a text saying he didn't agree with my lifestyle but that he still loved me. And he still wished I told him.

I am so much happier now that I'm not hiding who I am. I have a great relationship with my family. My mom gives the best advice on dating. I was having this problem with this guy once and my mom was just like "Rickey, some guys can just be jerks. You gotta love yourself before you love anybody else." And so I try to follow her advice, but that doesn't mean there aren't things I struggle with.

My dad and I still don't talk about me being gay. There was that one text message about it and that was it. He's coming around, though. And even though he hasn't fully come around, he is an amazing man and still supports me in everything I do.

I haven't yet introduced a guy to my family. I had a boyfriend and my dad didn't know. It was a serious relationship and he met my mom and he wanted to meet the rest of the family and all I could say was, "not right now." It's a hard thing when you're dating to not feel like you can bring a guy home. It's always in the back of my mind when I'm looking to be in a relationship. I feel like that's my dream. That's what I'm working toward. To someday meet someone who I am truly in love with and who truly loves me and someone who I want to introduce to my family. But I think it's a process. I know I'll get there.

Looking back, I wish I had been more comfortable to come out sooner. I still think that I'm sorry my family had to find out the way they did. I wish I told them before I moved to Los Angeles. Then, even if they had kicked me out, I was already leaving. I paid my own bills. I would've been okay.

And I wish I could tell young Rickey, *Hey, don't care about what other people think. Don't pretend you're someone else, just so you won't get hurt. Just be yourself and you will be happy.* Because my younger self would have been happier if he wasn't hiding. Even now, I've only really been out for like a minute. Dating guys is different than dating girls, and it's still all fresh and new for me. I think if I had come out sooner I would feel more prepared. Maybe I'd be at that point where I could take a boyfriend home.

But you can't come out before you're ready. If that's something you're struggling with, don't let anyone force you to come out. I'm not gonna lie, it was hard at first. Telling my friends, telling my family, not knowing how they would react. But then it just got easier. It really does get better. You may be sitting here like, *Yeah, whatever*—I know when I first heard people say that I never believed them. It's okay if it takes you a while. But right now just know it is okay to be you. If you love somebody, you love them. It's who you are. It's not a disease. It's not wrong. If people in your life hate you for being you, then you don't need them. You will find people who love you for you, no matter what. And if you feel like no one else is here with you, I am.

Cheap Booze and Old Lady Lipstick

I was fourteen years old when I was offered my first drink. It happened at a family friend's Bar Mitzvah, and it was *poppin'*. There was a DJ who only played disco and blink-182, a bar for the adults, and a lot of dads dancing. But the boys I knew weren't dancing; instead they were looking for alcoholic drinks left on tables, and they found them. Tons of them. Apparently people don't care as much about finishing their drinks at an open bar.

So I followed these boys to the underside of a table in the back of the room and watched as they finished those drinks. A couple of them had had alcohol before, or at least said they had, trying to be *cool*. Two others were going to try it for the first time, so I watched as they sipped a glass of something orange with lipstick still on the rim. They made disgusted faces, then passed the glass around. When it got to me, I froze. That was the first time I really felt peer pressure. I held the glass in my hand and looked at what I later found out was a screwdriver: vodka and orange juice. Then I passed it to the next kid without ever lifting it to my face.

No one noticed. No one called me a sissy, or held me down and forced me to drink it; they just kept drinking themselves. I was lucky not to have to deal with more extreme peer pressure, and it was then that I decided I was never going to drink.

To this day I haven't had a sip of alcohol. In high school, telling people that bit of information always led to curiosity. Most people asked if it was a religious thing. It's not. Others would ask me if I drank beer . . . *as if beer isn't considered alcohol? I don't know, drunk people aren't the brightest.* And sometimes peers would take my alcohol abstinence as a challenge, like "I'm going to be the person who gets Hunter to drink first!" But it never happened.

These days, as an adult, I usually get the opposite reaction. Telling someone that I don't drink is usually met with respect. People will tell me that they're jealous, that it's a waste of time, or they'll compliment me on my willpower. But honestly, it didn't take much willpower at all; it just took me looking at the people closest to me. My family.

First off, my grandmother. She was beautiful, smart, loving. She was an amazing cook, a skilled seamstress. She was an artist, a gardener, and a handywoman. She could fix anything and hang wallpaper like a boss. But I never got to meet her, because she was a severe alcoholic and cigarette smoker who died before I was born.

Alcoholism is not a weakness; it's a disease. It has nothing to do with willpower. It doesn't matter if those affected are successful actors, Nobel prize winners, political leaders, or a single mother of two like my grandmother—when an alcoholic starts drinking, they can't stop. It's just how the disease works. And it can be hereditary.

I see similarities between myself and my grandmother, little things that I've tried once and can't quit. For example, I know it's not the same, but I can't have just one Thin Mint Girl Scout Cookie. I also can't stop biting my nails. And believe me, I've tried everything under the sun: I've put bitter polish on my nails that tastes like old feet, but in the end it would

To this day I haven't had a sip of alcohol.

just make my mouth taste like old feet. I've snapped myself with a rubber band every time I raised my hand to my mouth, but that just hurt . . . a lot. I've even started getting my nails done with my girlfriend to curb this uncontrollable habit. Nothing works, and although it may not be a fatal habit, the fact that I can't stop still scares me.

Ever since I was young, the idea of drinking scared me for the same reason. There was this mental dam separating me from a wave of alcohol, and if I unplugged it for just a sip, everything else would come crashing down. I was so sure in my head that I would become an alcoholic. And even though I never met my grandmother, I saw what addiction could do to good people when my mom remarried when I was five and we moved in with my three new brothers: Eric, Bryce, and Curtis.

Bryce, six years older than me, was always looking out for us. He played video games with us, threatened to beat anyone up who messed with us, and had the biggest heart you could imagine. And I thought I would have that forever, but I didn't.

Bryce and his brothers had an anger inside them from their parents' divorce and it affected all of us. As a way of rebelling, they started making horrible decisions, which led to addictions. At the time I didn't know what they were doing, but I saw it break my stepdad and mom down and tear apart the family.

I would listen to these shouting matches between my parents and my stepbrothers regularly, until the day they were kicked out of the house for good. After that, I rarely saw my brothers. The few times I did see them, our relationship was different, if there at all. But with

But for me, the benefits are very heavily outweighed by the *what ifs* of it all.

Bryce I always believed the brother I knew was in there somewhere. I could see it underneath his tattoos, and his toughness, and I really wanted him to come back. But years later, when I was a teenager, Bryce went to prison. He got out, only to be sentenced again, this time for eight years.

Early last year he was released from prison and I finally got my older brother back. And the rest of my brothers are all on track now too. But that time in between, where they were gone from my life, will always be a reminder for me to not drink alcohol.

Sure, I know there are plenty of adults who can have a glass of wine with dinner or a drink with friends after work and be okay. And that's totally fine. But for me, the benefits are very heavily outweighed by the *what ifs* of it all.

What I'm trying to say is, rather than sit under a table smelling cheap booze and old lady lipstick, it probably would have been more fun out on the dance floor. Even if the DJ was playing "All the Small Things" for the fourth time.

Nothing Is the End

Rebecca Black

For as long as I can remember I just wanted to perform. I started dancing at three, and by the time I was nine I was in a performing group where we went and performed at military bases and retirement homes in funny little costumes! No matter what the outfit, though, I loved being on stage. I felt like I could do anything up there—not in the sense that I thought I was *so great*—but I just knew that that was where my heart was.

I had this solid idea of what my life would look like, and that life would be on Broadway. It wasn't a *maybe*, it was an "*I'm going to do this*", so I started on my path. First I went to El Rancho Charter School, known for its music and arts programs, where I immediately got into the musical theater program. I was only in middle school when I started looking at colleges like Juilliard and NYU. I had dedicated my life to musical theater. And getting the role of Laurey in my school's production of *Oklahoma!* was the achievement I was waiting for. It was supposed to be an exciting moment. I had auditioned for it, worked so hard to nail that lead role, and I had won it. I was on my way to my dream!

And then literally a week later "Friday" went viral and everything changed.

The irony of "Friday" going viral is that no one was supposed to see it. I had made this music video so I could say on my applications to Juilliard and NYU that I had experience in a studio and on-camera. I wasn't going to actually show it to anyone—maybe one of my grandparents who couldn't make it to my shows at school, but that was it. And then the company who made the video posted it online. Someone sent it to Tosh.0 and it went from 3,000 views to over 200,000 overnight. I came home from school one day and it was just there. And by the time I saw it online myself, it had taken on a life of its own. I remember someone saying to me, "you suck, but you're going to be famous."

If you don't know the rest of the story of "Friday," you can Google it. I'll wait. It's all out there on the internet forever—all the harsh things that happened. Before "Friday" happened I wasn't popular or unpopular. No one knew who I was. I was just Theater Girl. But after "Friday" everyone knew who I was.

I was terrified that all of a sudden all the work I had put in, all those vocal lessons, dance classes, and years on stage would be delegitimized in three minutes and forty-seven seconds. All I could think was that no one would ever take me seriously as a performer or as an artist. It was like all of my plans were suddenly out the window.

When it first happened I was in shock, and all I could do was sit on my mom's bed and cry. I remember she said, "We can call them and take the video down and it will all go away." But for some ridiculous reason, I looked her dead in the eye, and said *no*. There was something in me that wouldn't let all of these people win that easy. A few weeks later, it's like there wasn't even an option to take it down. It had become my life.

There was a good year following that where everything in my personal life became quite difficult. My grades dropped tremendously and I got crazily close to failing while all the people in the industry around me just kept telling me, "this interview is more important, you can do school later." By the end of the year I missed so much school I was afraid to go back. I dropped out of my prestigious musical theater program—me, Theater Girl, dropped out. I felt like me because I was in my own body, but it was almost like I had gotten stuck, and I stopped growing as a person. All the feistiness that I had, just dissipated. I could put it on when I walked into a meeting or an interview, but in my real life I was realizing I was beaten down. I would tell myself hey, *it's going to be fine,* but I wasn't actually sure.

There was something in me that wouldn't let all of these people win.

It wasn't until I finally graduated high school and moved to LA that I started to do things my own way. I stopped listening to everything that other people said I *needed* to be, and I got back to who I *wanted* to be. Once I started feeling more like myself, all of a sudden the things that I didn't know how to get rid of just melted away. I started working with people who helped me find aspects of me that had been buried under the turmoil of "Friday." And just as suddenly all these opportunities started popping up.

On some level we all have these moments when we realize things might not work out the way we planned. Whether it's parents getting divorced, being rejected from your dream college, not getting invited to a birthday party, or releasing "Friday." Large or small, when you're going through them they often feel massive because they mean that the future you wanted no longer seems possible. In the moment they feel like obstacles, but sometimes obstacles become gifts. You just have to see them as part of the journey rather than as derailing you.

Through all of this I found a stronger passion for something and achieving my dreams feels even more possible. I just moved out on my own. I've been working in the studio with producers and co-writers who encourage me to find my own spirit, this inspires me to write my own songs, to tell the stories I want to share. Sometimes it's terrifying, and scary, but everything I write in my new songs is *me*. I know that I took a strange path to achieve my goals of being a performer, but I got to where I wanted to be, just not how I expected. So if you're feeling like it's the end of the world, keep going.

Nothing is the end.

STILL NOT THE END

Congratulations! You've done what I could never do, finished a book. Now you are left with only three options:

1. READ IT AGAIN. Books usually go by too quickly. A paragraph becomes a page, a page turns into a chapter, and a chapter turns into the rest of the book. We often get so caught up in certain stories that others fly by without us even noticing. And when life is really hectic, many miss entire chapters! So take a deep breath,

2. SHELVE IT, AND COME BACK LATER. There are stories that you know will put a smile on your face, keep those nearby for the rest of your life. But every once in a while, we turn the page to a story that we're not quite ready for. A story that's just too painful to read at that exact moment. Those stories aren't skipped, just saved for a day when reading it won't hurt as much.

3. GIVE IT TO SOMEONE ELSE. Eventually you will have taken everything you can from this particular book. You'll look back and remember the time you spent with it during your highs and lows, but you'll know that it's time to move on. Then you'll hear one friend tell you about their troubles, and the book that you're holding in your hands, the one with dog-eared pages and your scribbles in the borders, will end up in theirs, and the process will begin again.

But again, as Rebecca Black said, this isn't the end, because books *don't* end. Instead the author just decides when to stop so that you can finish the story, and TBH, your story is incredible.

—Hunter

Acknowledgments

Don't click away just yet, these are the people that made this book happen.

First, thank you to all three of my parents. You have supported me since I surprised you with my existence. Without you, this book would not be here, and neither would I I love you.

To my girlfriend (or fiancee or wife or widow depending on when you're reading this,): I love you as well. You've given me more stories than I can fit in a single book, that's why I'm really hoping there's a sequel.

And thank you to the rest of the book's contributors, long-time friends and people who I met through this wonderful project. You've all made this book an incredible experience, and I really like you . . . sorry, it's just that love is a bit strong especially for some of you that I just met.

Next, my high school English teacher Michael Gross. You showed me that English was so much better than Math and Science, that's why this book is full of stories and not equations. You also bought me and my classmates books when we couldn't buy them ourselves, and thus are the reason that this book is doing the same for so many other young people. These books are being donated because of you.

Moving on, I want to thank my bosses Joe Davola and Brian Robbins. They gave me my first break when I was just a funny-looking kid with a silly YouTube channel. Now I'm a funny-looking kid with a silly YouTube channel, a book, and two incredible mentors.

To Scholastic, Debra Dorfman, and specifically Marisa Polansky my editor, thank you for believing in me from day one and more importantly, thank you for making sure I didn't spell anything wrong. Thank you to Suzanne LaGasa for her art that brought this book to life, and to Nora Kletter for all of her help with everything.

And finally, here are a bunch of people that said they would buy the book if their name was in it: Dylan, Ira, Dee Dee, Emily, Meredith, Morty, Reef, Sal (those last two are dogs), Lauren, Brett, Tara, Byron, Lisa, Scott, Brent, Erin, and Oprah.

I don't personally know Oprah, I'm just hoping she buys this book and puts it on a particular list . . .

YOU GET A BOOK!